The Germans in Trinidad

The Germans in Trinidad

Anthony de Verteuil, C.S.Sp.

THE LITHO PRESS
P-O-S., TRINIDAD

ISBN   976-8136-39-1

First published in 1994,
by Anthony de Verteuil, C.S.Sp.,
and printed by Litho Press.

MAPS, DIAGRAMS, SUMMARIES.

COVER ILLUSTRATION.

The Cover illustration has been executed by Maurice Chang. It shows the arms of three German States from which the chief characters in this book originated:

Hesse: Lion rampant - Urich & Boos.
Wurttemberg: 3 Panthers - Stollmeyer.
Rhineland: Horse & symbols - Leonard Graf.

The eagle is the symbol of the Federal Republic of Germany.

ILLUSTRATIONS.

INTRODUCTION

This book was originally intended as an introduction to the URICH DIARY, an extensive document of about 200 pages written by Friedrich Urich between 1830 and 1832, and which is perhaps the most important non-official document for Trinidad's history at that time. However, as the 'introduction' expanded, it became necessary to separate it off as a complete book in its own right, and this is what is presented here. It is hoped to publish the diary next year.

From the point of view of social history, the German element was fully integrated into Trinidadian society by the start of the Second World War, and so with a few exceptions, family histories are carried up to 1939 only. This book, however, is NOT meant to provide a comprehensive list of Germans who lived or settled in Trinidad. I apologize in advance to those who are disappointed at not finding the name of their family included here. In general, a fuller treatment is given to those families which emigrated to the island before 1875 or which were not involved in business, since businessmen, however admirable and hardworking, are not frightfully interesting to the average reader.

I wish to thank very sincerely the many families who entrusted their precious records to me, and for all the help and encouragement they gave. I am grateful to those at the Public Library and National Archives, the Archbishop's Archives, the Archives of the Anglican Church and Trinity Cathedral, who rendered assistance. Detailed acknowledgements are made in the notes at the end of the book. I thank particularly Mr Rene Bermudez who allowed me to reproduce photographs of the Siegert Family in his possession. Special thanks are also due to Aquarela Galleries and Mr Gerald G. Watterson for permission to reproduce paintings and sketches.

Messrs. Ian Jardine and Adrian Camps Campins have contributed in no small measure to the making of this book into a well-rounded production, by their sourcing of material, many valuable suggestions, and their reading of the manuscript. I am deeply appreciative of their kindness.

The book was typed by the author, and composited by Fr. Ronald Mendes C.S.Sp. who also designed the layout. The cover design was chosen by the author to indicate that this book is a companion volume to "Sylvester Devenish and the Irish in 19th Century Trinidad" and perhaps to other books yet to come. The art work was done by Maurice Chang. The negatives for the photographs were provided by Scrip-J and printing was carried out by the Litho Press. Many thanks to all those involved in the technical production.

I trust that the reader will enjoy the perusal of this book as much as I have enjoyed the preparation of it.

CONTENTS

CONTENTS

Chapter 1

The German Community

It is a matter of perfect indifference where a man originated, the only question is: "Is he true, in and for himself".

George Wilhelm Friedrich Hegel.

An attempt was once made to turn Trinidad into a German colony. The Great Elector of Brandenburg (Prussia), Friedrich Wilhelm, was determined to make his principality into a great power within the Holy Roman Empire (the forerunner of the Confederation of German States) and he began by seeking to establish naval superiority over the neighbouring states, based initially on a strong commercial fleet. In 1680 he sent a squadron of five ships to the Caribbean in search of prizes. They had little luck in capturing any merchant vessels and had to dispose of their few captures at Jamaica or at the French West Indies. Then, about the same time, a fort was built on the Gold Coast for the Brandenburg-African Company to begin slave trading with the West Indies. Friedrich Wilhelm entered into alliance with King Louis XIV of France and with his permission sought to establish a trading post in Tobago, but the States General of France successfully protested that the island was their property. Friedrich then tried to persuade Spain to cede Trinidad to him in

payment of an outstanding debt to Prussia, but
his offer was haughtily refused by the Spanish,
and so Trinidad did not then come under German
rule.

Yet a little more than a century later, in
1797, the Germans came to Trinidad as conquer-
ors. On February 18th when the British General,
Sir Ralph Abercromby, landed in Trinidad with
eight thousand men and took the country from the
Spanish Governor Chacon with the loss of only one
man, it was the Germans who led the attack on
the Laventille hills, and of the nine Regiments or
Detachments in Abercromby's force, the German
contingent was by far the largest. Hompesch's
Regiment was composed of 25 officers, 7 staff, 40
Non Commissioned Officers, 16 drummers and 773
men in other ranks. Lowenstein's Regiment had
13 officers, 6 staff, thirteen N.C.O's, 6 drummers
and 276 from other ranks, and like Hompesch's
regiment had been privately recruited, the mer-
cenaries coming in the case of Brigadier-General
Hompesch's regiment probably from Hanover. (In
1714 the Elector of Hanover, George Louis,
through his mother had ascended to the throne of
England as George I, and subsequent kings of
England were also rulers of Hanover, until in 1837
with the death of King William, Victoria, his niece,
succeeded to the throne of England, while in
Hanover, because a woman could not by law sit
on the throne, William's nephew Ernest became
ruler there). Some of the Hompesch Fusiliers, we
can take it, were recruited also from the princi-
palities of Nassau and Brunswick or Hesse, not

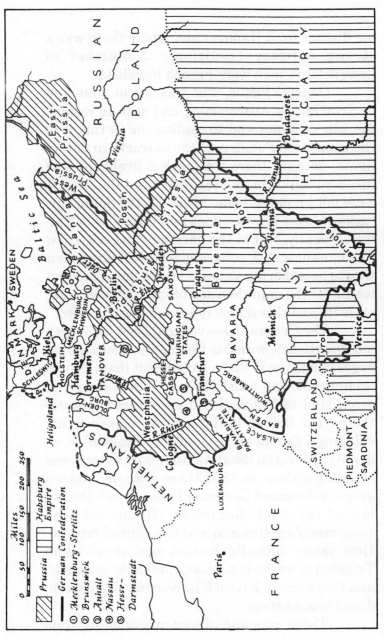

The German Confederation in 1815

too distant from Hanover and where there was a strong military tradition.   A number of Lowenstein's men were French Royalists.

General Picton, who was left in command in Trinidad by Abercromby, had soon to restrict the sale of liquor and to confine the Germans of the Hompesch Fusiliers to the barracks in Port of Spain, because there was such a lively spirit of insubordination in that regiment. But the soldiers were not prepared to die in the Port of Spain barracks of "slow fevers, agues and fluxes" which affected nearly half of the garrison, and not a few Germans deserted, some apparently finding their way to neighboring Venezuela. Picton offered rewards for the apprehension of missing men, alive or dead, and this seems to have had some effect.

The General however could not have been too dissatisfied with his German soldiers, for he suggested to the British Government that German soldiers who had finished their term of service be given land in Trinidad and encouraged to settle there. The British Parliament were keen on developing a European peasantry in Trinidad in order to cut down on the slave trade, and so approved of Picton's plan. In 1802 there were in Trinidad over one hundred Germans from the 5th Battalion of the 60th Regiment (Hompesch and Lowenstein's regiments) who had applied for land. How many actually settled and survived in Trinidad is anybody's guess - probably very few - and they seem to have left no recognizable descendants behind them.

There was one officer, presumably from

Lowenstein's Regiment, who remained on in
Trinidad and acquired land in the Maracas district, namely Baron de Boehmler. De Boehmler
was from Alsace, (a province near the river Rhine
and which at various times shifted from French
to German control) and probably a Catholic. Like
many a French member of the *noblesse d'epée, he*
had been forced to flee for his life from the Revolutionaries. His sword was passed down to the
eldest son, from generation unto generation. In
1832, Urich, one of his fellow Germans, referred
to him as "a German - a poor man, though rich in
pride". The de Boehmlers married into the French
creoles but showed an unusual aptitude for technical work and an exceptionally early willingness
(for a French creole) to work in the British civil
service, - beginning in the 1820's, one was a road
construction engineer, in 1914 Frank de Boehmler
held the post of District Officer, Public Works for
Princes Town, and his father before him occupied
a similar post at Couva.

In 1802 Trinidad was ceded officially by
Spain to England, and apparently at this stage
German traders began to settle in the island. In
1808 a German apothecary of Frederick Street,
Dr. Schaw, became notorious. He is reputed to
have entered an outhouse with a lighted candle
and accidentally set fire to some wood shavings
and straw. The flames spread rapidly to a
neigbouring store of nitrates and essential oils and
in the resulting conflagration 9 blocks of the town
of Port of Spain and all the public buildings were
burnt. (It was too a policeman of German extract,

Goring, whose carelessness led to the burning down of Police Headquarters in the 1880's!) According to the population census of 1810, out of a white adult population of 1,890, 25 were German-born, presumably some being merchants. A number of them, like Schuler, Dieffenthaller and Faltini had perforce to marry Catholics - if they wished to marry a white person, for the few Protestant Englishwomen favoured their own countrymen, since the Germans (justifiably or not) had a reputation for beating their wives.

If Leveingstein was his real name, and if he was a German, he was certainly no credit to his country. He appeared in Trinidad in early 1822 and visited the Temple of the Lodge United Brothers (*Les Frères Unis*) at Piccadily Street, with letters of recommendation from Masons and Lodges in the north Caribbean islands. He claimed he was a lancer from Napoleon's "Old Guard" and had fought in Russia in the snows of that terrible winter and against the British in the Emperor's last stand at Waterloo. He had then fled to Cuba, where he fell into the toils of the Spanish Inquisition and suffered greatly. With incredible ingenuity he managed to escape, and had been helped by the masons in Barbados, St Vincent and Martinique. He had, however, embroidered his story too much, for a few of the Roman Catholics in Lodge United Brothers knew that there had been no tribunal of the Inquisition in Cuba for more than forty years. Further investigation revealed that Leveingstein had swindled the Masons in the other islands. He was immediately expelled from the Trinidad Lodge (and the home of the mason with whom he had been staying) and letters were sent to all the Lodges in the Caribbean warning them about this confidence trickster.

By the mid-1820's there was an increase in the number of German merchants operating in the island, out of the capital, Port of Spain, - the Gerolds (who soon brought out their relatives Urich, Wuppermann and later Feez and Zurcher), the Bocks, the Mullers. Meyer, Schack, Schumann, Schulz, Fraenzl, and Schuler the cemetery keeper, also formed part of a small German group in the town but almost all have left no descendants bearing their name in Trinidad. There were, moreover, a number of technicians from Germany who were brought out by these merchants, a shoemaker, a gunner, a *fac totum*, as well as young clerks or overseers, who in those days of rigidly stratified society had a much lower social status, and their names have not come down to us, for most probably returned to Germany (as indeed many of the merchants seem to have done.) There were at one time or another a few Germans in the employ of or associated with, the Government, namely Von Weiler, Faltini (from Wurzburg, and in Trinidad from 1803, as a road engineer), Eckstein (born in England of a German father, a graduate of Rostock University and official translator in the Trinidad Courts) and possibly others. According to the Port of Spain Gazette of the 28th February 1827, there were at that time 34 German persons in Trinidad, 25 men, five women and

4 children. Interestingly enough, in the following year when the island's population was 48,994, the white population was 4,326, so that roughly every one person in twelve was white and every hundredth white was German, but their financial importance was far more than their numbers indicate.

Speaking German among themselves but also French (since this was the most widely spoken language in early nineteenth century Trinidad) and some English, for many years the Germans remained as a loose community in the island, middle class, well educated, Protestant, mainly city merchants and generally apolitical. For the first generation it was usual to return to Germany to get married, but after that the second generation married English creoles (who like them were Protestants) or wed Catholics, the Irish or Corsican creoles rather than the French creoles.

It was only towards the end of the nineteenth century that the German creoles became fully integrated into the French creole society. Indeed, the first (and by far the earliest, 1863) to marry into one of the prominent French creole families was Adolpho Wuppermann, who was Catholic (his mother being Zoyla Gomez from Angostura). And even he complained that: "Our good and beloved brother-in-law, Phillipe O'Connor died on the 28th November 1872... At his funeral I was refused 'crepe'(the black arm-band worn by close members of the deceased family) by his brothers." In a few cases, one member of the family might marry a German or German creole and another a

French creole, resulting in great cultural differences between the cousins, as aptly described by a liberal Lutheran cousin from Germany visiting his relatives, shortly after the First World War.

> I liked my Catholic cousins a lot better than the Protestant ones, they were like sisters to me and affectionate ones, none of that stiff calvinistic style, which took a kiss to be a mortal sin. Maybe if they enjoyed a kiss too much they just confessed it, did penance and that was it; while the protestant ones had to fret about such like matters for endless times, poor dears.

For the Germans, business was business. The French creoles, on the other hand, considered it was a mortal sin for one French creole to foreclose a mortgage on another - though of course there were sinners! As the Germans married into the French creole society there was an interaction of attitudes but eventually the German viewpoint won out. Here is a business letter written in reply to Joseph Gioannetti, (the legal agent for Mrs. Adolpho Wuppermann, née Ganteaume), who was dunning for a debt.

Arima 25th March 1907.

Dear Mr Gioannetti,

I got your letter and think that I shall be able to pay back to Mrs Wuppermann the four hundred dollars due her.

I have not been able to pay any interest as I was very hard up. I have not made forty bags of cocoa this year - I expect to do better in April-

May & June. Anyhow I will pay you the interest
due early in April - as soon as I shall have sold
my first lot of cocoa.

  We are fairly well. Presseni still continues
to suffer from her old complaint. Kind regards.
Yours Sincerely,
Louis Seheult.

  Sir Ralph Woodford, who was Governor of
Trinidad from 1813 till 1828, was very favourable
to the so-called "Aliens", the Spanish, French and
German settlers. When he was laying out Marine
Square (Independence Square) and Brunswick
Square (Woodford Square) he had them planted
with flowering trees specially selected by the eminent German Botanist, Baron Schack, who happened to be resident in the island at the time. But
with Woodford's death in 1828 official attitudes
changed. The question arose of introducing British law, and a new Constitution, promulgated in
December 1831, led to the exclusion of all "Aliens"
(foreign born citizens) from the Council of Government. The Aliens were deeply disturbed and sent
a Petition to the King of England pointing out that:

> As your Majesty's petitioners have spent the best
> part of their lives so they are desirous to con-
> tinue for the remainder of their days under the
> Flag which has protected them so long.... (they)
> respectfully pray ... to have such measures rec-
> ommended as will permanently secure the ad-
> mission of Your Petitioners into the great Fam-
> ily of Your Majesty's British born subjects.

  Because of this political uncertainty, and

much more because of the severe economic down-
turn consequent on the coming emancipation of
the slaves, the year 1832 probably saw the German commercial presence in Trinidad at its height,
and it declined for many years thereafter.

Some German names which appeared on
the petition above, were as follows: Juan Descovich
(an Austrian), Charles Schulz, Phillip Wehekind,
A. Gerold, A. Wupperman.   The list of Assessors
for Criminal Prosecutions for Port of Spain in 1832,
(reputable citizens of a certain standing) yields
other names: John Fanovich (Henry Street),
Antoin Dieffenthall(er) (Queen Street), Peter Witz
(Duke Street). It is perhaps a useful and interesting exercise to examine the history of some of these
early German settlers, and especially those who
have descendants in present-day Trinidad.

The Gerolds who first came to Trinidad,
Christian and Anselm, were the most unroman-
tic, skinflint businessmen one could meet and yet
their coming to Trinidad had about it an air of
magical coincidence. Things fell out in this fashion. The winter of 1812, was one of the coldest of
winters and on one particularly bleak Sunday afternoon, as a coach with one passenger was travelling through the village of Eschau in the district
of Hesse in Germany, it capsized and the passenger was thrown out and broke her collar-bone. This
unfortunate Madame Hugon was at first taken to
an inn and then through the kindness of the Al-
derman of the town, Christian Gottfried Gerold,
was brought to his own home to be cared for.
Madame Hugon spent three months in the warm,

hospitable bosom of the Gerold family, sharing
their joys and sorrows and fascinating them by
stories of life in Trinidad, where she ran a general
store with her husband. Europe was then in the
grip of the Napoleonic wars and the Gerolds had
just lost their eldest son fighting in Russia. Soon,
the other Gerold boys might be conscripted and
sucked into the conflict. When the time came to
leave, Madame Hugon in an emotional burst of
gratitude begged the Gerold couple, "Let me take
your sons Christian and Anselm to the West Indies
with me and save them from the chaos reigning in
Europe at present. We have no children as you
know. Let them be like sons to us and when we
retire in the not too distant future, they can take
over the flourishing business." Shortly after her
departure, Christian Gerold, followed a few years
later by his brother, Anselm, sailed for Trinidad.

After Christian had worked eight years in
the business, he demanded to be made a partner
in the firm. Eventually, in 1828 Hugon sold out
completely to the Gerolds and returned to France.
The business that the Gerolds controlled in 1829
was considerable. They lived in the large general
store situated at the western corner of South Quay
and Chacon Street. In fact, the front of the store
did at that time actually open out on a quay and
the sea, and a small row boat was kept in the yard.
The Gerolds also owned three sugar estates in the
Naparimas - Reform, Mon Chagrin and Matilda
(to the north and east of San Fernando) all acquired through the failure of their debtors. For a
similar reason they had an interest in a small
estate in Carenage. They also owned Copperhole

at Monos and were involved in the trade in whale oil. They brought out their close relatives to help in the business (see family tree on page 71). Both brothers returned to Germany to get married and then came back to their adopted home, Trinidad. In spite of various vicissitudes (notably bankruptcy in 1918) the Gerolds continued in business in Port of Spain. Edward Heinrich Gerold, grandson of Anselm, died in 1960, and his descendants are still alive in Trinidad today.

In 1830 the Gerolds invited their two nephews, Friedrich and Wilhelm Urich, to come out to Trinidad. The history of the Urich family in Trinidad is given in a later chapter.

Adolf Christian Wuppermann was the son of Christian Gerold's sister, Wilhelmina, and George Friedrich Wuppermann. As early as 1450, the Wuppermanns lived in Barmen, on the banks of the Wupper, (hence their family name) an east bank tributary of the Rhine. In 1503 Johann Wuppermann owned the 'Wupperhofes' (mansion or court at the Wupper). By 1700 the Wuppermanns were merchants in Barmen and among the first in the manufacture of silk cloth, which began about 1750. They lived some 80 miles from the Gerolds' home town and presumably had business associations with them. Adolf came out to Trinidad to work with the Gerolds in 1832. In 1834 he opened a business in Venezuela and married Zoyla Gomez at Angostura, where eight of his ten children were born - all to be brought up as Catholics. The three boys who survived to adulthood were George (who married Josephine Hancox and settled in New York, his son Francis becoming a famous film star under the name Frank Morgan); Eduard who wed Anna Sturm and lived with his three daughters in Germany; and Adolpho.

In 1850 Adolpho, then age ten, sailed from Angostura to Bremen. For the next six years he lived with his uncle Anselm in Frankfurt and attended classes at the Institute of Scheib and Geisor. He was then apprenticed to the House of Kettenheimer and finally spent 1860 with Rabone Bros. and Co. in Birmingham, England. In 1855 his paternal grandmother had given him a book embossed in gold, *"Tagebuch von A.Wuppermann"* for him to keep a diary. She wrote (in German):

Dear Adolpho,
Even though you are still at the happy age when events of life don't crowd and jostle each other and don't seem so serious and important, it would be nice and useful to write down on these pages what happens to you, and ponder about it. It is not the numerous and extraordinary events of life that shape our character and give meaning to and enrich our impressions and knowledge but **how** we experience them... On this journey of life take with you my blessing and be assured of my fondest love.
                              Your Grandmother.

In 1861 Adolpho came out from Germany to Trinidad to join the firm of Urich and Feez. Then, as he wrote in his diary: "on the 11th September 1862 I engaged myself to Miss Marie Ganteaume de Monteau," and "was married to Marie, 8th August 1863". Only five of their children survived to adulthood. Jerome, the elder son,

emigrated to Cuba. Georgiana, born in 1881, never
married and was for long years the President of
the Catholic Organization "Les Amantes de Jesus".
When Adolpho, a merchant all his life, died aged
47, his younger son Rudolph was only four years
old. He entered St Mary's College at age eleven
and with considerable guidance from his friend
Canon Doorly (of Queen's Royal College!) won an
island scholarship in 1902. He studied medicine
at Edinburgh University (with financial help from
his uncle George in New York). Of his University
days, he wrote: "We worked hard during lessons
but had some wonderful holidays cycling (on push
bikes) in the Scottish Highlands, the English Lake
District, Holland, Belgium and the Rhine district
of Germany." He spent time with his uncle Eduard
in Germany but did not like the country. He
claimed that the only two German words he
learned were *Verboten* (forbidden) and the word
for 'a trip on a ship', *Dampfschiffahrt*. Having
qualified, he returned to the Government service
in Trinidad in 1909. He married Anne Marie
Pantin, their children being Peter (who married
Gemma Maingot and settled with their family in
Florida), Marie Anne (Mrs Harold Mahon), Jean
(Mrs Sydney Knox), Angela, and Rosemary (Mrs
Joseph Herrera).

Of the Wuppermann's relatives (by marriage), Edward Feez, who had become a partner
in the firm of Gerold and Urich, married a Massy,
and spent money lavishly in various investments
and in travelling to Europe. When the firm failed
on the 21st May 1872, Feez found employment as

chef de bureau at Messrs Agostini, Smythe & Co. But by 1881 he was at death's door in his little home in St Anns, and his wife ran a book shop to try to earn some money. He died without male issue. Fritz Prahl of Lubeck had married Antonia Wuppermann, Adolpho's sister, in 1874 and set up business in Ciudad Bolivar. In 1880 he went into partnership with Adolpho Wuppermann in Trinidad, but this was dissolved a few years later and apparently the Prahls returned to Germany.

The Zurcher family originated in Switzerland, the name originally being *Zuricher* signifying a person from Zurich. They left Switzerland and settled in Illzach, a village near Mulhouse, which was at the time a free town allied to Switzerland. At the beginning of the nineteenth century, the family owned a factory for the printing of cotton goods at Cernay, a town near Mulhouse. One of the sisters of Anselm Gerold married Edward Feez whose sister had married Emile Zurcher of Mulhouse and it was their two sons, Emile and Fritz Zurcher, who came out to Trinidad in the 1850's to join Gerold and Company. Soon the Zurchers founded their own Company trading with Venezuela and Fritz Zurcher became part owner of the coconut plantation at Manzanilla known as the Cocal. Emile married a Dick (in 1858) and Fritz a Cumming (in 1860), both marriages being celebrated at the Anglican Trinity Church (now Cathedral), in Port of Spain. Emile had nine children but all died without male issue, except his son Emmanuel, whose son Emile was the last male member of the family in Trinidad.

Emile was one of the pioneers of petroleum production in Trinidad. He founded a company with a small refinery and produced his own gasoline under the name of "Silver Ray", but after a bitter price war, the multinational companies forced him out of business. Meanwhile Emile's first cousins (the children of Fritz) had emigrated to England, so with the death of Emile in 1958, the name of Zurcher vanished from the island and is only known to today's generation of Trinidadians because of a street in the town of San Fernando named in honour of his father Emmanuel Zurcher, who had been the Town Clerk of the southern metropolis. The following account in which Emile Zurcher is mentioned is self-explanatory.

Criminal Sessions - Tuesday 10th June 1856.
The Queen Vs J.P.Richardson, F.Kirk and Pancho Cuteris, charged with having on the 8th day of March last, stolen one heifer the property of Salvador Riza. Paul Latour - he is the keeper of the Queen's Park (Savannah), and as such, had in his custody, in the month of March last, a heifer marked with a brand **J**. He missed the heifer during that month and made enquiries about it. He went to the slaughtering establishment of Messrs Gerold and Urich in Corbeaux Town (Woodbrook) and saw Mr Zurcher there. Some hides were shown to him and he identified one of them as being the hide of the missing heifer.
John Richardson and John Kirk, guilty, 2 years imprisonment with hard labour.

The Von Weilers originated from the borders of Switzerland and Germany, (the prefix Von

indicating noble descent). They held Government
posts throughout the nineteenth century, for example, inspector of schools. The only Von Weiler
alive in Trinidad today is Eugenie Marie (mother
Maude Scott, paternal grandmother Ana Girod).
But though the Von Weiler name is forgotten in
Trinidad, the German genes remain in Mrs
Eugenie Marie McCarthy's 23 grandchildren and
40 great-grandchildren.

The Wehekinds were from Alsace. From
1667-1825 they were centered on the town of
Reguisheim. They were Catholics and when faced
with the 'aristocratic' French creoles in Trinidad,
apparently resurrected the legend (which they
themselves only half-believed) that they were descended from the famous 8th century Saxon Chief,
Wittekind. Phillipe, the first in Trinidad, (judg-
ing from the contents of letters he received from
Europe at that time), seems to have come out on a
visit concerned with legal or financial matters; but
he was enchanted by the island and remained on
as a music teacher. He was very much part of the
German group but unlike most of them, held that
there was no "German nation" but only a "German people". He married Adèle Leotaud in 1829,
and became a businessman. Five of their daughters and three sons survived to adulthood. Eugène
married an English lady with a French name, Dora
Mathieu, had one son Edouard, who remained
single, and four daughters who married into the
Aché and de Labastide families. Johnny, a confirmed bachelor and expert fisherman, held a lease
on Huevos island. The youngest son, Vincent Léon

Wehekind, born in 1856 in Port of Spain and educated at the newly founded St. Mary's College,
became a solicitor and vice-president of the
Trinidad Law Society. He married Matilde
O'Connor but died at the early age of fifty-one,
leaving three daughters, who married into the
Leotaud and Agostini families, and one son
Ludolph (1895-1964). Ludolph worked for the
asphalt Company in Venezuela and for more than
20 years as hydrologist with the Trinidad Government. He had no formal training as a naturalist
but was a born scientist. He was commissioned to
make a collection of fish for the Academy of Natural Science in Philadelphia and in the process discovered a new species of fish, named after him
Thalassophrynae wehekindi. He assisted
Friedrich Urich with his work on vampire bats and
was an expert in herpetology (the study of snakes).
He joined the Field Naturalist's Club in 1931 and
was later its President over a period of ten years.
Like his father, he was quite a talented artist. The
Wehekinds, unlike most of the other German families, were Catholics and immediately integrated
with French creole society. They preferred not to
be known as Germans.

Fanovich, (or Fanovitch) as we have seen,
was an assessor in 1832, and probably like
Descovich, of Slavic descent from the Austrian
Empire, and possibly associated with him in busi-
ness. They were Catholics. Around 1870 Andriette
Fanovich married Albert Ganteaume. Her brother
Luis was the Station Master at St. Joseph. On
the 28th January 1885, on the Trinidad Govern-

ment Railway, there was an unfortunate railway
accident near Champs Fleurs, a passenger and
luggage train colliding. Two people were killed
and several hurt. An attempt was made to make
a scapegoat of Fanovich. He was prosecuted for
manslaughter but the case was dismissed. His
descendants still live in Trinidad.

Shortly after the emancipation of the slaves
in 1834, the British Government made a grant of
£25,000 to the Church of England for building
school houses in the West Indies. The Church
Missionary Society (CMS) shared in this grant.
Under CMS auspices and on land given by the
Government, the Reverend Mulhauser (and the
Rev. Eckel) set up schools in San Fernando and
Savanna Grande. By 1842 there were three German clergy working in Trinidad, one at Savanna
Grande, one in the outskirts of San Fernando, near
Oropouche and one as assistant curate in Port of
Spain. The Germans were reportedly men of indefatigable zeal, preaching assiduously, but un-
fortunately in the case of one of them even the most
attentive congregation had extreme difficulty in
understanding what he said, because of his thick
German accent. It was largely through the efforts
of the Rev. John G.Mulhauser that the first Anglican Church was erected in San Fernando and
named St Paul's.

Mulhauser was energetic but had his full
share of German inflexibility and was willing to
fight not only against the Roman Catholics but
also against the Baptists and the Government. In
1836 he wrote to his superiors in London: "I would

De Boehmler Sword. Handle and upper blade.

The sword, (27.5 inches in length) is a light military sword of the type used by a subordinate commissioned officer, for fighting and signalling the troops. It is of a continental design with a stag-horn handle and typical of the late eighteenth century. The rose emblem is probably purely decorative.

The Wuppermann property at Barmen. 1826.

Rudy Wuppermann sent this old family sketch to his mother from the S.S.Maraval on 28th July 1903. On the back of it he wrote:

When Time that steals our years away
Shall steal our pleasures too
The memory of the past will stay
And half our joys review.

Then talk no more of future gloom
Our joys shall always last
For Hope shall brighten days to come
And memory gild the past.

Rudy Wuppermann and friends at Edinburgh University (1904)
Rudy back row, right; others in picture are Armand Pampellone,
Venancio Maralejo, Henry Fratz, Frank Greaves, Gordon Deane,
Andrew Krogh, Paul Guiseppi.

Being at University together helped to break down social barriers
on return to Trinidad.

The Zurcher home, "Blarney", just outside Port of Spain.
A substantial, well-designed home, situated on 20 acres of land in the present Ellerslie Park,
it was later acquired by the Rapseys and renamed "Ellerslie".

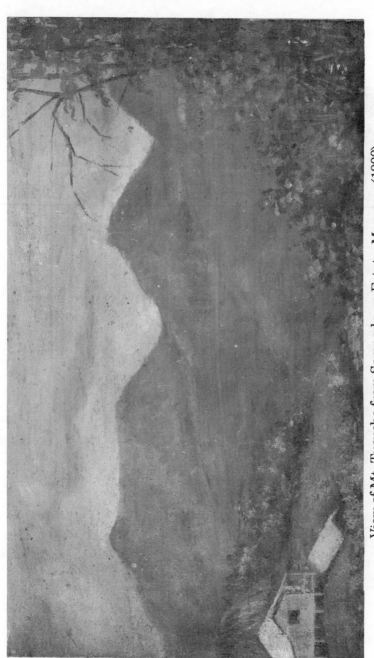

View of Mt. Tucuche from Sampadrura Estate, Maracas. (1900)
The family estate, painted by Léon Wehekind, a pupil of Cazabon.

Easter Card from Venezuela by Ludolf Wehekind

have no objection whatever to omit our Catechism (from school) but if they (the Government) will **forbid** to teach it by a **must** .... I do oppose such an intrusion and insolence". Fortunately, he became less intolerant as time passed. The newspapers recorded that, on the 16th of February 1840, he gave "a discourse in German at Holy Trinity Church for the benefit of the fifty odd Germans in the Congregation" - for indeed there had been a sudden influx of Germans into Trinidad.

With the end of the apprenticeship system in 1838, there resulted a great shortage of estate labour in Trinidad. Various plans were suggested for bringing in immigrants, including immigrants from Germany. The unrest in Germany consequent on the revolts in some states of the German Confederation in 1830 and the following years, and the great increase in population, as well as the consolidation of the great estates in Prussia which made many peasants landless, created a lower class susceptible to belief in promises of a new and rosy future open to them in the West Indies. Speculators willing to trade in human life found ready cooperators in estate owners desperate for cheap labour.

According to Carlton Ottley, "the immigrants were crowded into the holds of the sailing ships under conditions not entirely dissimilar to those experienced by the slaves in the Middle Passage," less than two score years before. The captains were concerned only with getting their human cargoes to Trinidad alive, so that they might receive in return the passage money for those who could find employment. Advertisements were placed in the press:

> Port of Spain Gazette, 3rd June 1839.
> 262 immigrants from Havre, France, in "la Jeune France" - Captain La Porte - in forty-two days. They are wishful of gaining employment as domestics, mechanics, or otherwise, either on the estates or in town. For further particulars apply to Captain la Porte at the Counting House of McAllister & Co. of King Street.

During the last three months of 1839, three French ships arrived from Le Havre with 676 French and German immigrants, in response to glowing advertisements about Trinidad posted up in that port. The passengers would sign a contract to work for an employer for three years, on condition that he would refund the cost of passage to the shipper e.g $55 - and then reimburse himself by withholding from the labourer his wages for two months each year. Most of the Germans (some of whom were sidetracked from New York and Philadelphia) were placed on the estates. They were considered to be "without distinction or education" and lived in the old slave huts. The newspapers reported of these European immigrants (mainly French and German): "The mortality among them occasioned by the fever and other tropical diseases to which they are afflicted is very high". From June 1839-June 1840, the Public Hospital, newly founded by the Town Council of Port of Spain, had been occupied by 615 patients of whom 427 were Europeans. Many of the immigrants took to drink or became vagrants.

Still the ships kept coming, because the captains felt they could make large sums of money by the planters paying for the passage, - and this indeed some of the cocoa planters were willing to do. In the 1840's there were in Trinidad 681 cocoa estates producing 3 million pounds of cocoa annually, but they paid lower wages than on the sugar estates. The estate owners hoped that European labourers might survive in cocoa cultivation, if not on the sugar estates. But the Governor was against the Europeans working on the cane estates. He wrote to the Secretary of State for the Colonies in 1839: "It is upsetting (whether to him personally or to the general population is not stated) to have Europeans and Negroes working in the cane fields together".

On the 21st March 1840 the sloop *Elizabeth* arrived in Port of Spain with one hundred and forty Swiss and Germans. On the 15th May another ship arrived from Le Havre with 190 French and Germans. The Governor, Sir Henry MacLeod, panicked. On the 29th May 1840 he wrote urgently to the Secretary of State for the Colonies:

My Lord,
It is my duty to request You Lordship's attention to the condition of the European immigrants who have arrived in this island in considerable numbers during the last six months...
I regret extremely to acquaint Your Lordship that nearly the worst apprehensions that could have been entertained for these people have

beenrealized.

I have ascertained that in the short space of four months there has been a mortality of upwards of 10% - very many more cases have occurred which we have not means at hand of ascertaining... lead me to fear still greater mortality. But it is not loss of life alone which has made this immigration peculiarly distressing.

The principal demand for their labour lies in the field. The employment is new to them, and their constitutions are unsuited to exposure to a tropical sun - sickness ensues - the estates of this Island are yet without those conveniences and comforts which a European looks for when in bad health .... many of these people, the Germans and the Prussians, being unable to speak the language of the country, are, when overtaken with illness, in a very forlorn and helpless condition.

Instances have occurred, but I am glad to say they have been rare, in which the master has not only declined to maintain his servant when overtaken with sickness and unable to work, but has cast him loose on society in a state of suffering and perfect helplessness. On the other hand, as would be expected, these immigrants are not always of good description... This latter portion of these people has afforded some instances of vagrancy, and many people have become a serious burden to the community in town, either in the shape of beggars or as suffering from disease.

Your Lordship may judge how shocked I was by the arrival here on the 15th inst, of another ship, the *Louise* from Havre, having on board 190 German and French people...

I have directed that none of them should be allowed to establish themselves here until they should first find surety, that for twelve months to come, they should not become destitute, or become chargeable to the Public...

But to put a stop to this traffic in human life, I request Your Lordship's assistance. In the case of the *Louise*, I have protested against the exaction of the passage of each immigrant of more than twelve dollars ... this may go some way towards checking further speculation of the kind...

I entreat Your Lordship will be good enough to take the necessary measures for calling on the French Government not to permit any vessels to clear from their ports with emigrants to Trinidad at least in ignorance of the disadvantages and other evils with which they will have to contend here...

I would respectfully suggest that a like communication be made to H.M.Minister to the Germanic Confederation...

Because of the Governor's action and because the planters quickly realized that the Europeans could not make suitable field labourers, whether on sugar or cocoa estates, this unfortunate immigration soon stopped - but not before it had led to enormous human suffering. To give but one instance, the case of Adam Ston, a German fifty-eight years old, who disembarked in Port of Spain in 1840, accompanied by his wife Phillipina 51, his daughters, Phillipina 25 and Elizabeth 24, his son Adam and his two grandchildren Nonne 2 and Madeleine 6 months. Because of his age, Ston could find no employment. He was unable to pay for the passages. Accordingly he was taken to court and convicted, and lodged in the debtor's prison in the Royal Gaol despite his fervent plea to be allowed to pay the passage money in installments.

For want of some place to reside, his wife and family were forced to live on the sidewalks of the town, and during the day had to solicit alms for their sustenance. Nothing further is known of the Germans who immigrated at this time. Most of them probably died within a short while or emigrated elsewhere, though as late as the Christmas season of 1842 there was an appeal for money to help a starving and sick German family.

After this tragic but short-lived episode in Trinidad's history, for some score of years there were few German immigrants to Trinidad, though one notable individual did arrive in 1845, Conrad Stollmeyer, and to him is devoted a later chapter.

The only other immigrant family before 1860 and the improvement in the Trinidad economy seems to have been the Borbergs. From at least 1350 the Borbergs had dwelt in Westphalia. Dr. Karl Borberg was a University professor and author of some 30 books, the most famous being *Das Leben Jesu (the Life of Jesus)*, in which he denied the divinity of Christ. He committed suicide in 1850, and his wife died shortly afterwards. Three of his sons, Adolph (b.1837), Otto (b.1839) and Emile (b.1843) were sent to Trinidad to join their uncle Reithard who had settled there some time earlier. Emile married Carolina Siegert; Otto never married, while Adolph wed Angela Hernandez and they had four children. The daughter Enriquetta married Joseph Llanos, and her brother Martin, by his first wife, had two children Emilio and Martin Adolph (whose family later emigrated to Barbados).

Emilio was expelled from St Mary's College at age 14. He later wrote: "In 1932 the population of Trinidad considered expelled boys and ex-convicts as dorgs with the same spots." After doing odd jobs for five years, including a stint on the Huggins' estates, he emigrated to Venezuela where he had a successful career and happy family life.

In the 1860's a new type of German immigration began, a number of German Roman Catholic priests coming out to Trinidad. By far the most numerous group belonged to the Holy Ghost Fathers and these will be dealt with under the chapter on Leonard Graf. Among the others a number were diocesan priests. The first, Fr.H.Flintoff, worked at Erin and La Brea from 1864 to 1867. A Fr.Francis Kums at Blanchisseuse in 1870 may also have been German. Albert Muller was Alsatian born and was parish priest of Cedros from 1879 till 1888. Conditions in Cedros were primitive, malaria was rampant, and what made it worse was that Muller had only to see the sea and he got sick. Hardly did he put his foot on the (weekly) steamer to Port of Spain, than he kept vomiting until he left it. He preferred to ride on horseback the score of miles from Cedros to San Fernando and then take the steamer from there. On one occasion he was in a small boat rowed by two men when the boat capsized off Erin and the priest barely made it to the shore. He then walked barefoot for miles along the rocky coast. At last, seeing a woman far off he hailed her, but looking at him and the hat of leaves he had made and with a palm branch over his head instead of an umbrella, she took him for a zombie and hid. Eventually he reached Erin. But Muller was strong as a bull; a fellow priest wrote of him: "The good priest has no doubts about himself. He has absolute confidence in his strength, calls the torrential rains beautiful weather, and fears the sea far more than the burning sun." But not caring for his health, after ten years, he was a broken man, and returning to Germany with his brother, he disappeared off the boat in mid-ocean.

Hubert Putz was born in Cologne, Germany. He became a Holy Ghost Father and taught for ten years at St Mary's College. But he hated teaching and was delighted to replace the parish priest of St Joseph for a year. He then returned to Europe and was told by the Superior General of the Holy Ghost Congregation that he was to stay in Europe. This he refused to do, left the Congregation and returned to Trinidad where he spent a year as parish priest of Princes Town. In 1899 the Archbishop sent him to St Vincent and he was a devoted pastor for over a dozen years. The one complaint about him was that he held a moonlight concert to raise funds for the church! Nearly aged sixty, he suddenly left St Vincent and got married before a magistrate in Barbados to a Vincentian girl. The marriage lasted only a few weeks and the priest realizing his folly abandoned his unfortunate wife. He did extensive penance and then wrote despairingly to the Archbishop:

Do, dear Archbishop, beg for me in Rome to be reinstated ... I should be outcast forever ... but the Saviour has promised forgiveness no matter

how deeply fallen, and he would have saved even
Judas if he had repented. Well I think I have
repented and sincerely.

He was reinstated officially by Rome, but
could not find a Bishop to accept him. Eventually
when he had begun ministering in Puerto Rico,
his wife threatened to pursue him there; the
Bishop asked him to leave at once and he fled post
haste to New York. Once again, he could not obtain a position any where, and the last we know of
him (from one of his letters) is that he was working "as a common labourer, moving goods of 300
pounds weight with lacerated hands."
Augustine Neff was from Alsace. He
worked in St Lucia and then came to Trinidad,
spending most of the 1880's as parish priest of
Santa Cruz. During the years he spent there he
was well known for his strict accounting of funds
collected and for paying off all debts on a yearly
basis. Leonard Meister, born in Bavaria, belonged
to the Order of St Augustine. He was ordained in
1898 and came to Trinidad from Dominica. He
worked in Couva, Erin, La Brea, Mayaro and
Maraval, from 1911 to 1915. Fr. Koos, a priest of
the Dominican Order, was born of a German father and an English mother, and served in the
parishes of Oropouche and Siparia from 1919 to
1924, ministering particularly to the East Indians. Born in Duren, Germany, in 1869, Fr.
Herman Schnitzler transferred to Trinidad from
Panama in 1928. He had a doctorate in Philosophy, the most painful rheumatism and (possibly
as the result of this) a terrible temper. He died

during his fourth year as pastor of the church in
Maracas valley and is buried in Lapeyrouse Cemetery.

Eugene Tritscher is the last German to
have served as a parish priest in Trinidad. He
was born in Lochwiller, Alsace, in 1886 and died
in 1962 in Port of Spain. He had been previously
a missionary in Martinique, then in Margarita and
finally came to Trinidad. He was pastor in a number of parishes in Trinidad: in Chaguanas, Diego
Martin and sixteen years in La Brea, from 1926-
1941. Unlike some of the other German priests in
Trinidad, he never mastered English completely.
At his death he willed all his possessions to the
St Vincent de Paul society and the St Vincent de
Paul House in Santa Cruz is named Tritscher
House in his memory.

Dutch Benedictines are usually associated
with the Abbey of Mount St. Benedict, Tunapuna,
but in fact a number of the priests and brothers
were Germans, namely, Fathers Paul Dobbert,
Sebastian Weber, Ludger Nauer and Brothers Joseph Kleinmann and Anthony Feldner, - as so
listed by Archbishop Flood in his report of the year
1919.

Paul Dobbert was a monk in the monastery in Bahia, Brasil, and was one of the three
foundation members of the Monastery of Our Lady
of Exile in Trinidad, sent from Brazil in 1912. He
served for a short while in the parish of Arouca,
along with Brother Anthony Feldner.

Sebastian Weber, born in 1880 and ordained priest on the 7th April 1907, came to

Trinidad from Bahia in 1913. He served in a number of parishes in Trinidad: Chaguanas (1923), Cedros (1924-25) and San Fernando (1930-1950). A most zealous parish priest, he immediately recognized the need for a Catholic Secondary school in San Fernando and with the help of Edgar Mitchell and Vernon Ferrer (two past pupils of St. Mary's College) he set up classes for thirty boys in the basement of the presbytery, - the beginning of St. Benedict's College (now Presentation College, San Fernando). The school's motto, eminently suited to the site, was: *Per ardua ad astra*, (Through hardship to the stars). He persuaded the Archbishop to buy "Colony House", the southern residence of the Governor in his visits to San Fernando, for £5,000, just in time to forestall its purchase by "a ring of High Street moguls." Fr. Weber was one of the official exorcists of the diocese and people came to him from all over Trinidad to cast out devils from those they considered possessed. After 20 years as Parish Priest, Sebastian Weber returned to the monastery of Mount St Benedict where he was elected sub-Prior and where he died on the 12th July 1954.

Ludger Nauer, the third Principal of St. Benedict's San Fernando, came from the town of Crefeld in the diocese of Cologne. He was born in 1894 and ordained priest on the 27th June, 1922. Having taught for a number of years at St. Benedict's College, during his tenure as Principal (1934-1939), the school was affiliated to Queen's Royal College, thereby receiving Government recognition. He started numerous extra-curricula activities ranging from debating to boxing and opened "St. Benedict's Home" which housed 18 boarders under the care of a matron. The school population was then a little under 150.

Brother Joseph Kleinmann was professed as a brother on the 12th December, 1897 and came to Trinidad from Bahia in 1912. He laboured manfully and faithfully at the Monastery until his death on the 20th May 1942. He built the fine altar in the present Chapel of Mount St. Benedict. Like the other Germans who were Benedictines, his essential witness was community life and prayer rather than the works which he accomplished.

By 1900 most of the German creoles in Trinidad were Catholic and a number of Religious were the sons or daughters of German creoles. In the Holy Ghost Congregation: Fr. Kevin Devenish, Fr. Anthony de Verteuil; in the White Fathers, Fr. John Boos; in the Congregation of St. Joseph of Cluny: Sr. Marie Dieffenthaller, Sr. Ignace Dieffenthaller, Sr. Mary Fanovich, Sr. Elizabeth Gomez, Sr. Francis Xavier Urich; in the Dominican Sisters: Sr. Catherine Emmanuel Von Weiler, (who worked for years nursing the lepers at Chacachacare).

Finally, on the 15th July 1966 German Franciscan Sisters of the Sorrowful Mother established the St. Elizabeth Clinic in Henry Street, Port of Spain, and operated it until, most regrettably, some dozen years later their unionized staff made such exorbitant financial demands on them that it became impossible for them to continue the clinic and they decided to leave Trinidad. Certainly, from the point of view of religion, the Germans in Trinidad have made an inestimable contribution which it is well to remember with gratitude.

As the economy of Trinidad picked up in the 1860's, the already existing German commercial Houses brought out other Germans to assist them, notably Schoener and Boos. Ludwig Schoener Von Stroben Hardt, from Erbach in Hesse, went as a junior to Urich and Co. Ltd.'s agency in Paris and then came out to Trinidad. He wrote home to his younger brother Auguste telling him of the life in Trinidad, outings to Blue Basin, the need to become a good brewer and to learn French and above all to beware of women - "here in Trinidad there are devilishly beautiful ones; but you must preserve your manhood". But neither Ludwig nor his brother, who followed him to Trinidad, were immune to the feminine spells! In 1869 Ludwig married Julia Scott, an English (Anglican) creole, their children being Marie, Miriam, Julia and Ludwig Henry (born in 1874). Of Ludwig Henry's five children only one, Eric, married a French creole - Hélène Lange.

Ludwig's brother Auguste, married an Arundel. Shortly after the birth of their son August, on the 16th December 1885 Auguste was chatting in his store with a fellow merchant Schaeffer, when he was shot at point blank range and killed by a lunatic, Benjamin Britton. Britton was courageously brought under control by a labourer, Isaac Wilson, but not before he had wounded two other people. Schoener's son August was educated in England and in the first World War was a Captain and Company Commander of the 8th Battalion B.W.I. Regiment. In 1914 for political reasons, the name of their firm, Schoener & Co." was changed to "Trinidad Import and Export Co. Ltd" and still exists today on its original site, managed by the descendants of its original owners.

The Franco-Prussian war of 1870 with the complete defeat and humiliation of France, the German acquisition of Alsace-Lorraine and the creation of the German Empire, caused a temporary rift between the French and German creoles in Trinidad and prevented the earlier integration of the latter. Sylvester Devenish, the French creole poet, wrote a number of poems, set to music, about the war, calling on France to "Trample underfoot the German avalanche", "Never submit to the Prussian Eagles"; and after the surrender of France, demanding "Vengeance and carnage". This ill-feeling continued on for at least a decade, if we are to judge from the following incident (recorded by Abbé Massé) which occurred at the Hotel de France in Port of Spain in October 1879. A German clerk said to his neighbour at table in a very loud voice so that the whole room could hear: "I detest the French". Immediately the reply came: "You are an insolent man, and when you detest the French you don't go to a Hotel called the Hotel de France and run by French ladies. It is because I am French that I speak this way to you." The proprietress of the Hotel, who was in fact from

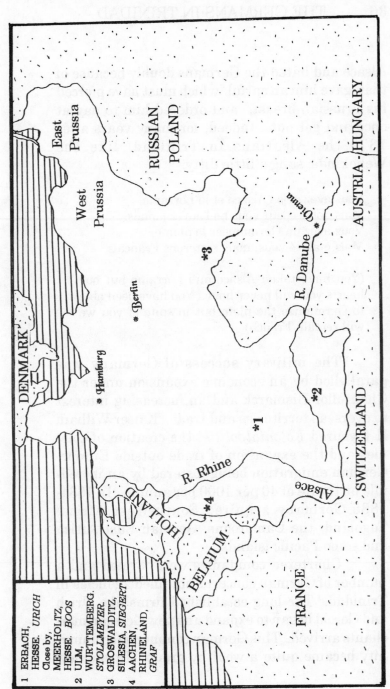

The German Empire 1870 - 1918

1 ERBACH, HESSE. *URICH*
Close by, MEERHOLTZ, HESSE. *BOOS*
2 ULM, WURTTEMBERG. *STOLLMEYER*
3 GROSWALDITZ, SILESIA, *SIEGERT*
4 AACHEN, RHINELAND, *GRAF*

Alsace and hated the Germans doubly because of
that, gave him an earful "which must have pierced
his Prussian breast," and ordered him to pay at
once and get out. Indeed, for many years after
1870 the Alsatians in Trinidad, like the
Wehekinds, sang a little ditty:

Vous avez pris l'Alsace et la Lorraine,
Mais notre coeur vous ne l'aurez jamais.
Vous avez pu Germaniser la plaine,
Mais malgré vous, nous resterons Français.

(You have taken Alsace and Lorraine but our
hearts you will never have. You have been able
to Germanize the plain but in spite of you we
will remain French).

The military success of Germany was
parallelled by an economic expansion under the
Chancellor Bismarck and an increasing interest
in overseas territories and trade. Kaiser William
II favoured *Kolonialpolitik*, the creation of colonies and the expansion of trade outside Europe,
German emigration being fostered by an incredible birthrate of 40 per 1000 per annum. In 1884-
1885 Germany acquired South-West Africa,
Togoland, the Cameroons, German East Africa
and some Pacific islands.

Chartered companies were formed and a
number of German concerns obtained agencies in
Trinidad. The long-established firms like Urich
and Gerold began to expand and new German merchants arrived. This German commercial community became quite a wealthy group. In the new

housing development in the area of present-day Tranquillity square, amidst 'streets of bright, well-built villas', they set up the Germania Club, (which reputedly had first occupied a rented house at Cotton Hill) where the German merchants could socialize and establish business contacts. A number of them availed of the new tennis courts at Tranquillity Square or sat amid the ornamental shrubbery there on a Friday evening to listen to the Police Band playing from 5 to 6 p.m. When early in 1883, H.R.H. Prince Henry of Prussia visited Trinidad as a naval cadet on the German cruiser *Olga*, he was entertained by the members of the Germania Club.

This German commercial presence continued to increase until the outbreak of World War I, in 1914. In 1911, there were 82 German-born persons in Trinidad and probably about 120 German creoles out of a total white population of around 4,000.

It was in the early 1900's too, that German and British warships in conjunction with one another frequented the West Indies in order to put pressure on Venezuela to settle its debts with their respective countries. Germany moreover, had designs on a naval station in the West Indies or even on a future canal through the Central American isthmus. Almost every month or two German cruisers or frigates called in at Trinidad or Tobago. Sometimes the officers were feted; on other occasions the ship's crew helped out in various ways; as for instance on the 5th August 1904 the band from the German cruiser *Vineta* gave a concert at the Princes Building, Port of Spain, in aid of local charitable institutions. As they marched or wandered through Port of Spain, the discipline and appearance of the sailors all helped to make Trinidadians of the time conscious of German efficiency and worldwide presence.

'The West Indies' by Macmillan, published in 1909, as also the Trinidad Reviewer of 1899, by T.Fitz-Evan Eversley, give some details of the German-owned firms then existing in Port of Spain.

Louis Scherer joined E.G.Gerold in founding a hardware store on South Quay in 1880. Paul H.Scheerer, agent for the Hamburg-American Line and cocoa merchant, was established in Charlotte Street in 1897. In fact, in 1909, one sixth of the 60 licensed cocoa dealers in Trinidad were German firms, the cocoa trade being then at the height of its prosperity: "Across the railway lines a huge shed with thousands of bags of cocoa with tracks alongside unloading; cocoa bags hustled down the shoots and wheel barrows roaring to and fro; cartmen of the lowest type cussing in the strongest language".

Matthaeus Leonard Goellnicht was born in Furth (near Nurnberg) Bavaria, from a family of mastercraftsmen and came out to Trinidad in the 1870's to the firm of Gerold. He married Catherine Mary Fahey (daughter of John Fahey and Mary Gruber) in 1880 and had two sons and a daughter. He died in 1893, aged 38. His older son, John Adam, born in Trinidad in 1881, was educated at Queen's Royal College and joined Gerold and Co. He married Lillian Arbuckle and had two boys and four girls.

Max Reimer, a commission merchant, shipped in cattle from Ciudad Bolivar. After trekking for considerable distances across the Llanos, they were put on board the stern-wheel steamers at Ciudad Bolivar, and packed so close that they could not lie down but spent the two days on board trying to gore one another to death. They were landed near Woodbrook and prepared by the firm for the Trinidad table. Reputedly the meat from them was as hard 'as though they had walked all the way from Venezuela'. Skeoch & Company were drapers, owners of the Klondyke. Wilhelm Holler (Consul for Denmark) and his brother August Holler, born in Hamburg, were merchants. Bernstein and Meyer (owner of the East End Foundry) were of German extract. Other Germans such as Speir and Mittelstaedt were employed in the commercial ventures in Port of Spain. Maritime and Fire insurance companies from Mannheim and Magdeburg had their agents in Port of Spain. Thor Schjolseth was one of them. He married Jessie Tucker, of La Cuesa, at St Chad's Chapel of Ease in 1879, and after her death, Bonifacia Siegert, who bore him three children, Carlos, Maria and Thor who was to become one of Trinidad's best known soccer players. Schaeffer owned and operated the Trinidad Chocolate Company.

F. Wippenbeck was a merchant in San Fernando in 1875. He seems to have married a German, had one daughter Juilliet and returning to Trinidad with his wife and daughter (presum-

ably from a holiday) his son Konrad was born on
the ship in 1901. Another son, Fred, died as a
teenager in Trinidad. The Wippenbeck descendants in Trinidad include the Byce, Main,
Fernandes and Hackshaw families. Konrad married a Foster and for long years he lovingly maintained 'the Castle', the old steam water-pumping
station in upper Diego Martin, where a marble
plaque was erected in his memory. He lived in a
little house, near the wells, beneath the shady
trees. Periodically (till he was stopped by the police, in the late 1940's) he used to ride his horse
into Port of Spain - a short, bald-headed man, in a
black suit, with blue eyes and a huge, red handle-
bar moustache, seated jauntily (and perforce un-
steadily) on old Rose, who sometimes, politely and
almost apologetically, dropped her calling card.

Indeed, it is difficult to overestimate the
importance of the German community in
Trinidad's business towards the end of the nineteenth century. Many of the major businesses
like Harriman and Gerold and Schoener were
German. Stollmeyer had begun to invest huge
sums in ventures like the telephone and Tram
Companies and paper making. A.S.Eckstein
headed one of the Free Mason lodges. The Cheva-
lier Hugo Hoffman, Consul for the German Empire, was in 1898, Vice-President of the Trinidad
Chamber of Commerce. Non-German merchants
like Miller, Archer and Agostini pursued courses
in business and technology in Germany and in a
few cases married Germans or German creoles.

From 1860, to the outbreak of the First

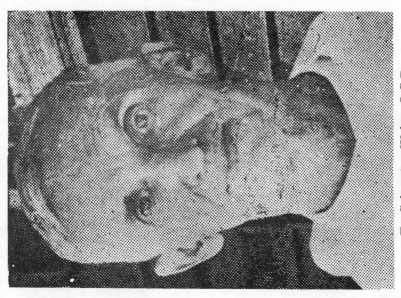

Fr. Sebastian Weber O.S.B.
Parish Priest of SanFernando

Emilio Borberg (centre) at Macqueripe Bay
with Percy & Dickie Huggins.

Ludwig Schoener Von Stroben Hardt 1843-1882.

Auguste Schoener Von Stroben Hardt 1853-1885.

The Germania Club, built around 1885.
Now, No. 12 Victoria Avenue.

The Wharf, Ciudad Bolivar, (1900) at the start of the Dry Season. Germans, often linked to Trinidad, controlled most of the trade.

Railway Accident at Champs Fleurs, 1885.
As a result of this, Luis Fanovich, the Stationmaster of St. Joseph, was prosecuted for manslaughter.

World War, in 1914, a general feeling of optimism and success had carried science in Germany to a height never since attained, especially in chemistry, physics and technological sciences. This fact was recognized in Trinidad and Germans were employed by preference in these fields. Germans were to be found in technical trades (in the broad sense), for example, C.O.Bock in pharmaceuticals, Ernst Vahl a watchmaker, Sauermann as an engineer, George Sieffert, an electrical engineer and manager of the London Electric Theatre, William Kramer, born in 1864, at Rottwell, manager of the Queen's Park Hotel, P.Strasser, Trinidad's first modern funeral undertaker, Felix Baccarcich (Austrian) in the police, and Selman, a recipient of the Iron Cross, (presumably in the Franco Prussian war of 1870) who married a Hart and had numerous children, including two boys, Franz and Elliot and two girls who married Andrew and Arthur Maingot.

The Hahn family originated from the island of Sylt, on the western coast of Denmark, which passed a number of times from Danish to German rule. The name Hahn, in German means rooster. In 1836 Dirk Meinertz Hahn was the captain of a fine vessel out of Altona, the *Zebra,* in which he once took a cargo of Huguenots from Europe to Australia. In subsequent years he plied between Trinidad and Carupano in Venezuela. The captain's son Dirk Dirksen (married to Henrietta Korngiebel) settled in Trinidad, continuing the trade with Venezuela, his only surviving son Daniel Meinertz being born in Carupano in 1867.

The young man was educated at Hamburg and at
the Polytechnic school of engineering in Berlin, and
after two years in England returned to Trinidad
to take up a post in the public works department.
On the 25th March 1904, in presenting the keys
of the newly built Queen's Royal College to His
Excellency, the Governor, the Director of Public
Works stated: "the credit for the building belongs
to D.M. Hahn, chief draughtsman, who prepared
the plans and with unwearied energy superin-
tended the construction."

Hahn also designed and built our present
Parliament buildings, the Red House. This was a
colossal undertaking. A contemporary account of
April 4th, 1906 describes it.

> Every day that one passes the Red House, one is
> struck more and more, with the great strides that
> the building is making towards completion - vast
> stores of wood work, cement, plaster of Paris
> friezes, cedar and mahogany panelling, sand,
> gravel and cement scattered here and there about
> - scaffolding everywhere - a little army of work-
> men. The Public Works Department is firm in
> its endeavour of finishing the work at the time
> stated.

The work was completed in time, by the end of the
year. The entablature and dais at the eastern end
of the Legislative Council Chamber, with its col-
umns of purple heart, as well as the Dragon (Sea
serpent), the wind vane, on the top of the building
(now defaced by a defecating dove or as some su-
perstitious people put it, "by a Battoo sign - we

boun' to dead!") were also designed by Hahn. He was responsible too, for the enlarging of the Victoria Institute in 1897, and for the building of the Mental Hospital in St Anns. He owned one of the first cars in the country and drove all over the island to inspect and build a number of bridges. For many years he lived in an extraordinarily ornate ginger-bread house at the corner of Queen and St Vincent Streets. In 1930 it was bought by Dr McShine and reassembled at 103C St Vincent Street.

Daniel married twice. By his first wife, Caroline Rose Baptista, he had five sons. One died young, whilst Fred (who won an island scholarship from Queen's Royal College), Henry and Bobby all studied engineering in England and settled there after graduating. Karl completed his medical degree in London in 1946, married and returned to Trinidad, but had no children. After the death of his first wife in 1903, Daniel married Olive Van Buren. The Van Burens, from the village of Bueren in Holland, emigrated to the United States in 1678, and after four generations of medical doctors, Washington Van Buren emigrated to Trinidad, where he married a Lake, Olive being their daughter. Olive had two sons, John, who died without issue and David Stuart, who was only eight years of age at the time of his father's death in 1933. Dave married Mary Lees of Nevis, daughter of Sir Arthur Lees, Baronet. Their son, Stuart, is one of Trinidad's better-known artists, painting in a semi-surrealistic style.

An unusual immigrant was Herr Christian

Wilhelm Nothnagel, born in 1867, at Altona, a small town near Hamburg in north Germany in the province of Schleswig-Holstein, just a year after the territory had been wrested from the Danes by the Germans. His father, Henrick George, was twice married. Caroline, his eldest daughter by the first marriage (born 1849) married James Miller of Trinidad; and in the 1880's, her younger sisters Johanna and Elizabeth came out to the West Indies to establish the newfangled Kindergarten schools, (a system invented in Germany in 1837, to educate children age 4-6 by means of play.) They established schools in Barbados, Grenada and Trinidad. Christian Wilhelm, the youngest of Henrick Nothnagels' nine children, did a three year course at Segeberg Seminary in the province of Schleswig-Holstein, qualifying him for teaching, with special emphasis on music, choral training and conducting and studies in the organ, piano, violin and cello. After qualifying in 1887, he taught for a few years at a Hamburg High school and then paid a visit to his sisters in Trinidad. He fell in love with the island and returned in two or three years time to settle there, helping at first in his sister's school, teaching music at Tranquillity school and (even though a Lutheran) filling the post of organist at Greyfriar's Presbyterian Church, Port of Spain, for very many years.

He married Dora Fahey (the daughter of John Fahey and Mary Gruber from Alsace) who had studied music at Frankfurt, and set up his own school of music at his residence, 18 Gray Street -

The St Clair School of Music: subjects: Piano,
Organ, Violin, Cello, Singing, Theory of music;
fees, $5 for 8 half-hour lessons; students' evenings
for playing before small audiences are held
monthly; students are prepared for Trinity College of music or London exams.

The school, founded in 1899, continued till
his death in 1932. He was appointed local secretary of the Trinity College of Music, and also became an agent for German and English piano
manufacturers, to help him support his family of
seven boys and one girl. He was the originator of
the choral and instrumental (Amateurs' Orchestra) section of the Victoria Institute, and a very
popular entertainer.

He lived for his children and for his music.
He wrote in 1927, when the new-type gramophone
finally reached Trinidad, expressing the beauty
and wonder of recorded music (which we now take
so much for granted):

"Nobody can quite know what this gramophone
means to me. The Music which it can reproduce,
used to be part of my life, and for 37 years I had
to miss it. I tried to fill up this gap by the Institute Orchestra, but it is so imperfect, and so is
the Police Band, compared with the effects I get
from the gramophone and the beautiful
orthophonic records - in the comfort of my own
home. I am very grateful to you Otto (his son)
for having offered this as a gift to me".

At Christian Wilhelm's death, the papers
reported:

Prominent officials of the Colony, leading members of the mercantile world, and a representative gathering of all walks of life in a mile long procession of motor cars, preceded by the hearse and three motor cars laden with magnificent wreaths, marked the respect paid to one of Trinidad's greatest musicians yesterday... With the exception of Archdeacon Doorly, no man has done more for the advancement of music in this island than he did. One can hardly remember any grand concert held here within the past quarter of a century in which Mr Nothnagel did not figure in some way.

Music was then, as it is now, a great unifying and exhilarating experience.

Of Christian Wilhelm's children, Oscar married Sheila McLean and had one daughter; Frank wed her sister Jessie and had one son (not married) and a daughter; Kurt decided to spend his life as proprietor of the Robinson Crusoe Hotel in Tobago. He did this so well (with the help of his sister Wanda) that he soon became known internationally. He was the epitome of elegance and kindness, as welcoming to the schoolgirl who came in for a glass of orange juice, as to the Bank Manager who dropped by for a scotch. The Hotel was a sort of cultural centre, and in the quiet times, was graced by Kurt playing the piano. His brother Desmond, for years a talented concert singer in Trinidad, wed Mary Cornelliac and they were blessed with one daughter. Otto, married to Roslyn Salazar had a son and two daughters. In 1948, Neils married Marie Antoinette de Gannes and had a family of two daughters, Voinceille

('Fritzie' - who continued in her grandfather's musical tradition) and Veilchen Julia, and three sons, Nicholas, Hans and Christian Wilhelm. The Benjamin of the musician's family was Harold (or Fuchie as he was known). An enthusiastic tennis player, he was four times singles champion of Trinidad and won the national doubles 14 times in combination with Cuthbert Thavenot. He married Helen Hunter and had four children, Elizabeth, Donald, Brian and Johanna.

There had been some German emigration to the West Indies other than Trinidad, in the nineteenth century and also to Ciudad Bolivar in Venezuela. The trade of this Venezuelan port, 240 miles up the Orinoco River was dominated by German families with commercial connections to Trinidad far greater than exist nowadays. Towards the close of the nineteenth century, a few coloured or white families of German descent came to settle in Trinidad. Perhaps one of the most notable were the Gocking family.

Gocking was a German resident in St Vincent in the 1850's, possibly a merchant and supposedly the editor of the local newspaper. In 1858 British sailors from the "Jasper" were involved in an incident one night in Kingstown and, typical of the time, returned the next night to take revenge. Gocking was one of the parties they injured, and he wrote complaining of the matter to the British Government. He was married to the illegitimate progeny of Sir Charles Brisbane, ex-Governor of the island, and was not to be taken lightly. He brought, like many another German immigrant, physical stature and immense energy to the West Indian population, reputedly having swum from St Vincent to the Grenadine island of Bequia, some five miles distant. His children, born in the 1860's - Charlie, Richard, Phil and Alice, emigrated to Trinidad in the 1890's. Charlie, who spent some years in the United States and was in touch with Marconi, worked for years in the cable office in Trinidad. In 1912 he was the Radio Operator on the little hill of Trois Amis outside of San Fernando, from which could be seen the sugar trains going to the refinery at Reform estate. He would sometimes go on horseback to the cable hut at Moruga when repairs were needed to the cable where it came ashore there. Of his two sons, William was the Chief Librarian of the University of the West Indies, and Dr. Vernon Gocking became eventually Educational Adviser to the Prime Minister and is the one mainly responsible for the institution of fifty scholarships based on the Advanced Level Cambridge Examinations and the maintenance of the different subject groupings.

George Grudden Dieffenthaller, born in Austria, migrated to Holland and thence to Surinam where he worked with the firm of Algemeen Nederlandsch Verbond. He came to Trinidad in the 1870's (being domiciled in San Fernando) and had three sons, Sydney, George, and Arthur who in the 1890's worked in Port of Spain as sales representative for George Polson, a druggist. He married Eva Guiseppi, who was the Headteacher at Mucurapo R.C. School. They had five children, the best known being Ray

Edwin. He went to school at St. Mary's College, and with the death of his mother entered the business world at the age of sixteen. In 1941, when he was 40 years old, he founded Hardware and Oilfield Equipment Company Limited, of which he was Managing Director for 49 years.

When he had to borrow money from the Bank as capital for the new company, Ray explained to R.B.McKenzie, the manager of Barclays, that he had no collateral. The latter replied: "Christ man, you will only fail if you die, and I have your life policy to cover that". Ray was "the great motivator", rewarding employees according to the efforts they made in the interest of the firm and not using the same scale for everyone. He took a personal interest in the welfare of his employees whom he regarded as part of the family business. He was a pillar of the Roman Catholic Church and of the business establishment of the country, working every day at hardware business for 72 years. But he was "first of all a gentleman". He received the National Award of a Chaconia medal in 1978. He was very proud of his large family; some time before his death, he had 21 grandchildren and 16 great-grandchildren.

Otto Hans Delzin emigrated to Trinidad from Venezuela in the 1890's. Wenzelmann was another German-Venezuelan as also the Siegerts. Carlos Schock, born in Venezuela of German parents from Hamburg and educated in Germany, eventually settled in Trinidad. After the death of her parents in Ciudad Bolivar, Zoylita Brumer (who had been educated in Germany) lived with

her aunt, Sophia Wulff, in Port of Spain. She was
to marry J.D.Lenagan and he describes how they
first fell in love. The setting was the magnificent
mansion of White Hall, built by Léon Agostini in
1903 and called "Rosenweg" (Path of the Roses) -
the light streaming from the windows, the carriages and one or two shiny new motor-cars drawing up, the ladies in their long flowing dresses,
with their escorts happily assisting them up the
steps, the garden in front bathed in quiet light
away from the music and dancing and laughter.

The 3rd May, 1913 was a most important day for
me. The Robert Hendersons of White Hall were
celebrating their Silver Wedding anniversary. I
was invited to the party and was at a loss to se-
lect a present for those wealthy people. My
mother gave me some old silver and I had a paper weight made in the shape of a lover's knot. I
little dreamt that I would be tied in such a knot
that night. Soon after my arrival at the party I
caught sight of a young lady whom I had met at
this house two years before. When I saw her she
was surrounded by a number of men all bent on
booking dances with her, and no wonder, for she
was by far the most beautiful girl at the party of
about 600 guests. By the time my turn came to
claim a dance, there was only one left. In due
course, my turn came to dance with her. After
our dance we sat in the garden. There was a
long interval. By the time the next dance struck
up I was madly in love with her. I could not let
her go over to her next partner. From our niche
in the garden we could see him pacing all the
verandahs, madly searching for her. I entreated
her to stay with me. She yielded, and is still with

me at my side, as I write this 40 years after. She was undoubtedly the *belle* of the ball and still is the apple of my eye. The guests that night had been supplied with fans. In my coat-tail pocket I found one that my love had used during the evening and wrote this little verse on it. Zoylita still has the fan.

> When this fan was stolen
> The hours were golden
> And happiness reigned in White Hall.
> While in me a feeling
> Was quietly stealing
> The heart which till then was my all.
> Now that I've tasted of heaven
> And the fan has been given
> To the angel who taught me to steal
> But I am yet to begin
> To repent for the sin
> That gave birth to the joys that we feel.

She left the party at about 2 a.m. with her aunt Sofia Wulff, her chaperon. I saw them off. I danced no more. From then until 5 a.m. I drank and smoked cigars. I had forgotten to ask my Zoylita where she lived! I left the party at 5 a.m. walked through the Grand Savanna to my home in Dundonald Street and tumbled into bed thinking of nothing else but the beauty I had met and how I was to manage to meet her again.

In the 1870's there were amazingly rich finds of gold at El Callao (east of Ciudad Bolivar) where at the height of its success original shares of 1,000 pesos produced dividends of 72,000 pesos annually. Other gold companies were formed by speculators, one of whom claimed later that "the richest of all mines, the best paying of all lodes is the credulity of the human race". Gold fever spread as far as Germany and among the adventurous young men who sailed to Venezuela, was Friedrich Wilhelm Meyer, born in Bremen around 1850, the son of Dr. Theodore Meyer. For months the young German camped in Guasipati on the border between Venezuela and British Guiana, panning and digging for gold - in vain. He settled in British Guiana for a while, married and then returned to Venezuela, - Ciudad Bolivar, this time - and set up a drug store in that city, where by hard work he made the fortune he had failed to find in the forest. He came to Trinidad about 1890 and purchased an acre of land at the corner of Jerningham Avenue and Belmont Circular road, where he built his home.   All but one of his 5 daughters and 4 sons were educated abroad, either in England or Germany.

Charles, the eldest son, wished to be a planter, and his father bought for him a coffee and cocoa plantation, Spring Hill Estate near Arima, (now the Asa Wright Nature Centre).   He married Julie Pouchet, so that all nine of their children were brought up as Catholics.   William, the second son, won an island scholarship from Queen's Royal College in 1895, and graduated from Edinburgh University in 1902 with an M.D. Ch.B. For years he was medical officer for Paria and Blanchisseuse. Patients slung in hammocks were brought to him by land and sea at all hours of the day and night. Later he undertook private practice in Arima. A visit to the doctor cost 24 cents and Dr. Meyer allowed the patients to take drugs on his account at the drug store opposite and pay him back later when they were well and could work again. Most got well but never well enough to refund the doctor! William married Frieda Opitz in Germany in 1912. They had 5 children. He died in 1935.

Robert, William's brother went to Glasgow Scotland in 1910, qualified as a druggist and married Jessie Brown of Glasgow. His father bought for him Laing's Pharmacy at the corner of Frederick and Prince Streets, Port of Spain. It was reputedly the first pharmacy in Trinidad to produce and sell aerated beverages. At the start of World War I, the Government confiscated the pharmacy. Frederick, the fourth son went to England in 1912 to study engineering. He married Elfriede Rosin of Germany and their son Peter became a pathologist. Of Friedrich William's descendants in Trinidad among the better known are Tom Meyer, (squadron leader in the R.A.F. in World War II and the late Head of the Fire Services in Trinidad), Carl A. Meyer (architect and insurance agent) and Lady Erna Reece.

Almost without exception, the Germans who emigrated to Trinidad in the 19th century worked extraordinarily hard, but many when the day's work was over drank hard, and not a few were unsuccessful in making the transition from German beer in their homeland, to gin, whisky, and rum in Trinidad; or perhaps they suffered from a hereditary pre-disposition to alcoholism. Moreover, they (or at least their young children) seem to have been particularly susceptible to the rav-

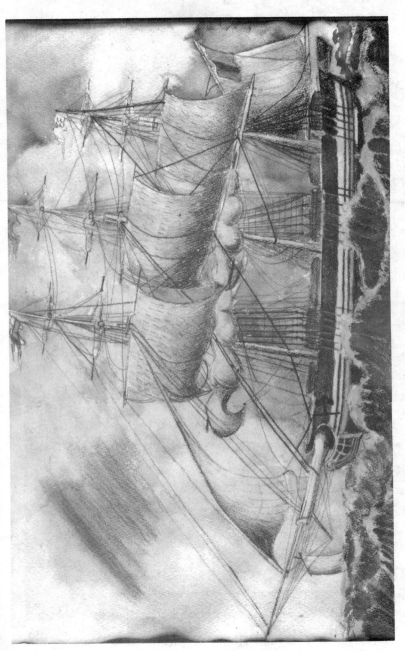

"The Zebra" (1842) captained by Dirk Meinertz Hahn.
A painting by Stuart Hahn, after an old lithograph.

The home of Auguste Holler at Queen Street, (1890)
just east of Abercromy Street. His business place was situated
at South Quay. By this date, it was no longer customary
to live above one's store.

Above: Musical Trio - Cello, Piano & Violin.
Christian Nothnagel, his wife Dora and Captain Schlimbak.
Below: Six little German Sailor Boys - all Nothnagels.
Oscar, Frank, Kurt, Desmond, Otto, Neils.

Friedrich Wilhelm Meyer 1850-1916.

William Meyer, graduate from Edinburgh University (1902).

Trinidad Fencing Club (1896) including a number of Germans. (l. to r.)

Back: E.Montenegro, I.Bodu, R.Torres, R.Bermudez, A.Pollonais, F.Camps-Campins, Rodriguez, Milk. *Sitting:* G.H.Mason, J.M.Bermudez, Schierholz, Quesnel. *On Floor:* Schock, Von Albrecht.

ages of malaria, dysentery and diphtheria. For instance in the case of Adolpho Wuppermann, born in 1840, in Angostura, and who married Marie Adèle Ganteaume in 1863, (apart altogether from a number of miscarriages), of fourteen children born between 1864 and 1885, only 5 survived, the rest dying of various diseases between the ages of 18 months and ten years. The poor father wrote in his diary:

> This terrible blow after all the losses of our other children cannot be written down - God's mercy is great and we pray to Him that He may spare us the other dear children. His intentions and His objects are impenetrable and as good Christians we have to bend to His Almighty Will and convince ourselves that it must be for our good that He demands all these sacrifices from us.... Our dear and beloved daughter May (Marie Sofia) died of pernicious malignant fever. God wanted her! What a grief to lose our eighth child! She was just 9 years old! To describe my grief is impossible; she died perfectly conscious. She confessed and Father Schmitz who attended her to the last moment said he never saw a child of her age die with such Christian resignation and with such profound religious sentiments. She is in heaven and has joined her 7 other sisters and brothers who went before her. May she invoke God's mercy for us!

Not surprisingly with such a high child mortality rate, in the 19th century there was little expansion of the German community in Trinidad, through natural increase.

On the 28th June 1914 Archduke Francis

Ferdinand, the Crown Prince of Austria, was assassinated by a Serb near the bridge crossing the river at Sarajevo, Bosnia. Within six weeks of the incident, war had been declared between England, France and Russia on one side and Germany and Austria on the other. The war was to completely destroy the expatriate German community in Trinidad. On August 5th an Order in Council placed restrictions on all Aliens. Anyone who was a German citizen (even though born in Trinidad) had to register with the police. On the 18th August they were required to reside in Port of Spain and not go beyond the city limits. "In the event of six guns being fired in Port of Spain and red flags flown at Public Buildings" they were to proceed with all haste to Police Headquarters, where they would be "safely accommodated". On the 3rd September the limits of their freedom were further circumscribed and some (with a Trinidadian wife and children!) were ordered to "leave this Colony forthwith". When this order was not followed, the delinquents were interned in the police barracks at St James. This internship was applied quite unevenly to the German creoles, some members of a family being interned, others merely having to report on a daily basis in Port of Spain. On October 31st a Proclamation was made prohibiting any business to be carried on in the Colony by or on behalf of any alien enemy.

A spirit of patriotism swept Trinidad. Hundreds volunteered to join the West Indian Regiments. Those at home showed their love of England by anti-German expressions. For instance, Nothnagel when teaching the children at Tranquillity school to sing "Rule Britannia" was greeted with a shout of "Kraut" ("Cabbage" - because the Germans loved sour-kraut). The headmaster of the Maraval school reported the Rev. Meister to the Governor for being pro-German; but his parishioners who hated the schoolmaster because he had publicly declared: "I never met a place with so many fools as Maraval", wrote to the Archbishop: "the Headteacher is himself for the Germans. He advised us when we enlisted not to go to the front as we were about to be crushed by the Germans and he is sure the Germans are going to win the war".

It has been impossible to discover the number of those interned. The treatment of some was tolerant, Nothnagel for instance getting regular passes for permission to be absent from the "Military Camp", to teach from 6.15 to 9.00 a.m. and 12.30 to 6 p.m. every week-day. Nevertheless, this placed a great strain on his wife and children who at times were practically starving, digging up their garden to grow vegetables and raising chickens to supplement their diet. Only one German was given a full days pass to continue his work in the city.

Others were treated more harshly and never given a pass to leave the camp. A number of escapes were attempted. One or two were successful. Warzes who had been arrested as he was having breakfast with his wife (a Trinidadian) and his son Charles, at their house opposite Tranquillity Square was taken unceremoniously to the Barracks. Charles (now a vigorous 96 years of age and a japanese judo expert) smuggled in a trowel for his father. He visited him frequently and each time he brought out with him a large bag of earth - for the guards did not think it necessary to examine what was taken out from the Camp. One day when he went to visit, his father was gone having tunneled out to the St. James river. Charles missed some clothes from his home that night but never saw his father again. Presumably he escaped to Venezuela.

The Trinidad Guardian of May 28th, 1918, carried the following report:

> The interned German prisoner Harry Jeste, who escaped from the St James Detention Camp on Saturday afternoon was captured the same night by Lance Corporal Clunes of the Diego Martin Police Station at 12 o'clock, in a small hut about half a mile away from the sea at the Diego Martin village. When under arrest the prisoner told Clunes that he made his escape by jumping the prison wall while everybody's attention was centred on the military sports which were going on at the barracks. He offered no resistance and was taken to the Diego Martin Station until Sunday morning, when he was taken to the Royal Gaol. As is usual, a court martial will be held shortly when the prisoner will be dealt with.

The threatening clouds of the 1914 war had forced a decision on some German creoles. In 1912, one branch of the Schoeners changed their name to Scott, the other to Arrindell, (after the names of their spouses); the Von Weilers now originated from 'the Swiss border', north or south of it not being indicated!   Several Germans fled to Venezuela, in the nick of time. For many years after the end of the war in 1918 Germans were not welcome in Trinidad.

As early as the First World War there were a number of Sephardic (Spanish speaking) Jews in Trinidad, the Senior, de Lima, Pereira and Herrera families. One German Jewish family, the Strumwassers (and a few other East European Jews) were established in the island before 1938; but that year saw an influx into Trinidad. In 1935 in Germany, Adolph Hitler passed a series of anti-Jewish laws including death for intermarriage with Aryans. Many Jews fled to Austria, but in the *Anchluss* (Annexation) of March 1938, that country was incorporated into Germany. Because no visa was required to settle in Trinidad but only a bond or deposit of £50, some of the hundreds of Jews fleeing Europe began arriving in the island, until the Legislative Council in early 1939 blocked further immigration by the refugees. Then the Second World War began. By February 1940, there were some 585 immigrants, including 300 'enemy aliens' (Germans and Austrians with a very few Italians) in the island and a decision was taken to intern them.

About 120 men (including non-Jews) were transported to Nelson island while accommodation was being built for them near St. James Barracks. The women (fewer in number) were held at Caledonia, another one of the tiny "Five Islands" in the Port of Spain harbour, and they remained there some short time after the men had been moved to the mainland. They spent their time stretched out in the sun, cultivating tans to escape boredom; while in the shade of a leafy Matapal tree on the neighbouring islet of Nelson, Tubal Uriah Buzz Butler, the riotous, Grenadian-born labour leader, sat sedately in his rocking chair, stroking his long beard and quietly oscillating his large fan. Eventually the women were united with their husbands at the internment camp. A total of about 340 people were interned, only about 40 not being Jews.

The camp, surrounded by barbed wire, with watchtowers and searchlights and guarded day and night, was situated in the present Federation Park. In *Camp Rented Trinidad*, as it was code named, families could live together in the long wooden barracks and there was "Home Rule" in the camp. The inmates organized things themselves, rosters for cooking or orderlies or camp cleaning. Arrangements were made for religious services and some families started vegetable gardens. There was football, table tennis, camp fires when personal stories would be swopped. The children were dropped to school in Port of Spain each morning by the authorities and picked up in the evening. According to Hans Stetcher, the younger people adapted successfully to confinement. Teenagers like himself were able to acquire numerous skills from the other prisoners, many of whom were highly educated and talented: higher mathematics, judo, watch repair or skills in leather work (with leather smuggled in wrapped round his body under his shirt which later helped Hans to set up a successful business in 1943 with an initial grand capital of $5.00 and forced to cut the leather on the floor for lack of a table!)

But the older people found life very depressing, especially in the early days of the war when the news from the front was bad. Because of the awful sense of frustration there were occasional fist fights. One university professor committed suicide by hanging himself. Every night all listened intently to the B.B.C. news and when some Allied victory was announced there were resounding cheers. It is indeed a really terrible thing to feel that Hitler's first victims, the German Jews (a few of whom like Schwartz and Karlsbad had escaped from concentration camps with their numbers already tattooed on their forearms) had to suffer three and a half years of internment in Trinidad. In May 1941, the *Winnipeg*, flying the Vichy flag and taking Jews (who had fled the Nazis) to settle in Santo Domingo, was captured by the allies and escorted to Trinidad. Huge Marquee tents were set up at the internment camp to accommodate the several hundred new internees, matters being complicated later by a burst water main. Good sense prevailed in 1943, and numbers of the internees were released.

Many German Jews remained in Trinidad to take up business. An attempt was made to get a permanent Synagogue built, either on lands owned by Averboukh (a Rumanian Jew who developed New Yalta at the entrance to Diego Martin) or on City Council lands at Mucurapo; but for reasons unknown though easily surmised, the City Council kept postponing consideration of the mat-

ter. The proposed synagogue site is at present oc-
cupied by the Jamaat Al Muslimeen mosque.
There was an exodus of Jews in 1970 to the United
States and Canada and at present only three or
four German Jewish families are still in Trinidad,
- Stetcher, Richter, Faigenbaum.

In the period between the two world wars,
to all intents and purposes the German creoles
formed a homogenous community with the French
creoles, though they still kept up business, educational and medical links with Germany rather
than England or France. German creoles more
and more were to be found in other than business
professions. A few, like Von Albrecht (champion
cyclist at the turn of the century before the ad-
vent of Mikey Cipriani) had always been prominent in sport, now they excelled in a wide variety
of sporting fields - names like Thor Scholseth in
football, Futchie Nothnagel and Herman Urich in
tennis, Victor and Jeffrey Stollmeyer in cricket
come to mind.

Between the two world wars a handful of
Germans came to Trinidad - Rudolph Fritz
Schneider, the grandson of a high-ranking German naval officer who was killed in the first world
war, Nils Voss who emigrated to Trinidad from
Stuttgart in 1926 at the age of nineteen, Chaim
Grossberg, Polish from Lodz but of German extract, Harry Reichmann from Magdeburg who
married Audrey Meyer, and a few others.

Considering the small number of Germans
who settled in Trinidad, they had a considerable
impact on the whole community, since they be-

longed to the influential white elite. At certain
periods, one in a hundred (or at very maximum,
in 1913 around one in 30) of the whites in Trinidad
were German or German creole, but they were
based in the capital, controlled considerable finance and counted among them some very outstanding individuals, so that the influence they
exerted was out of all proportion to their numbers.
Along with the French Huguenots they formed in
nineteenth century Trinidad an important bridge
between the Protestant English and Catholic
French creoles, preventing perhaps too bitter an
antagonism between them on religious grounds;
and their intermarrying in both groups brought a
welcome new stock of genes into the small white
upper and middle class.

Their attitude to work was quite unlike that
of the French creoles, organized and regular, busi-
nesslike and ready to undertake work of any kind
- even sewage collection! They brought new attitudes which were eventually accepted by the
French creoles - it became socially acceptable to
loan money to a brother who was in trouble rather
than to give, to save money was no longer un-
gentlemanly, better to be house-proud than to
spend money lavishly entertaining friends.

The Germans valued education and in
many different ways contributed to cultural and
scientific development in Trinidad. They were
prominent particularly in technical works and
businesses. From the religious viewpoint they
made an important contribution to the island. Had
they any special influence on racial relations in

the island? - is a question that may be asked but
is difficult to answer. Their one legacy to the local
cuisine is the continuing popularity of braun
among the French creole class - though some
people claim that Trinidad souse has a partly German origin. A few streets and houses in Trinidad
still bear German names. The Christmas trees
long traditional in Hesse (from which many Germans came to Trinidad) became popular also in
the island.

In Trinidad today, there are very few Germans, but our island continues to profit from German interest in the community. The German em-
bassy has been responsible for a considerable in-
put into social works and the German Roman
Catholic Bishops through *Adveniat* have helped
in the building of numerous churches throughout
the country as well as in the support of the local
seminary. It is well then, that we should be aware
of our German legacy and the importance of its
role in the building up of our country, and be grateful for the continuing help that comes to us from
across the ocean.

Chapter 2

The Urich Family

Much more happiness is to be found in the world than gloomy eyes discern.
Friedrich Wilhelm Nietzsche.

According to an old tradition, the Urich family originated in Switzerland. In 1888, Adolf Urich christened his new home at St. Anns, just outside Port of Spain, *Schweizer House*, that is, *Swiss House*. However, the records from Germany show that as early as 1606, the Urich family were established in the little principality of Hesse, (see map on page 35), at first at the village of Umbstadt and then a century later at the town of Erbach. This was in "the very heartland of the beautiful mountain region of the Odenwald and Vogelsberg, Hessen-Darmstadt and Oberhessen - each little town with its church, castle, framework houses with pious sentences carved into the beams, flower cases on the windows".

For some two centuries the Urichs were tradesmen or technicians - shoemakers, surveyors, marrying among their own social class; though in 1728 Johann F. Urich, then a shopkeeper but no doubt deeply pierced by Cupid's shaft, married perhaps just a little bit below his level, a blacksmith's daughter. After 1750, his son,

Johann Otto Urich, is described as a Burgher; and Otto's son, Johann Balthazar Urich, born in 1777, became a land law actuary and married Caroline Gerold, the daughter of the Mayor of the nearby town. They were blessed with nine children, five boys and four girls, and in spite of the very difficult times consequent on the Napoleonic wars they were all well educated, one of them, in fact, was to become a medical doctor. The outlook that was later to be described as *Bildung* (Education) was already in existence - it included feeling for scholarship and art and for overall intellectual and moral striving. This admirable, solidly middle-class, Protestant ethic the Urichs were to bring with them when they came to Trinidad.

In 1815 the German Confederation had been formed, made up of 39 mainly German States, but including Luxembourg and Czechoslovakia and excluding East Prussia (see map on page 3). This gave peace to Germany for half a century but it did not bring economic well-being. Bad harvests in 1816-1817 were followed by an economic crisis. In 1819 the Carlsbad decrees imposed rigid censorship on the newspapers. The rapid growth of population within the Confederation, (from 1816-1848, it increased from 24 to 36 million) put pressure on living space, the petty nobles recovered some of their privileges and the middle class underwent a sort of social demotion. The Urich family council decided in 1828 that two of the young men in the family, Friedrich Gottfried born in 1807, and his brother Wilhelm, just a year younger, should sail out to the island of Trinidad in the West Indies, to join their two uncles, Christian and Anselm Gerold, who ran a business in the capital Port of Spain, and that later they might possibly go on to the United States. And so, aged 21, Friedrich Urich came out to Trinidad, to be followed shortly after by his brother Wilhelm and his first cousin, Adolf Wuppermann.

Friedrich was a clerk in the Gerolds' General Store situated at the corner of Chacon Street and South Quay. In fact the store opened out on a quay and the sea, and a small row boat was kept in the yard. As a clerk in the store, the young man had a salary of £200 a year with board and lodging. This was no princely sum, as Henri Lequin, who was a clerk at the firm of Schultz, got £300 a year, lodging and a very good table. But at the Gerolds they never ate well, and Friedrich, who was a strong young man with a hearty appetite, always left the breakfast table hungry.

As was the custom then, the Gerolds lived above their store, which was on the ground floor. Urich however was at the back of the store, occupying a room which was more like a stable than a proper room for human beings. When it rained, he had to get out of his hammock to avoid getting wet. The roof needed repairing, but this was never done during the whole of Urich's stay there. The room itself was fifteen feet by twelve. It had one door with jalousies and on the other side it had an opening for air which was only one foot square. Friedrich usually slept in a hammock, because sometimes his uncles used to offer a bed to a good customer from the country and as there was no spare bed, the young German's resting place was allocated to the guest.

His uncles worked him hard. He generally rose at 4.00 a.m. and had only quarter of an hour for breakfast. He worked in the store from 6.00 a.m. to 5.00 p.m. and on occasion even later. A serious, studious, conscientious and ambitious young man, he quickly learned French and a little English and later began to study Spanish. He discovered much about the country from the old mulatress slave, Marie Josephine, who for years had been the housekeeper and was completely loyal to the family she served. When Wilhelm Urich, Friedrich's younger brother, came out to Trinidad, his uncles soon made him manager of a sugar estate, and sometimes Friedrich was asked to help with the running of the estate for a month or two.

Eventually, the Gerolds sent Friedrich to Angostura (Ciudad Bolivar) in Venezuela, with his cousin Adolf Wuppermann, where they opened a firm with R.Dick, a Scotsman, under the name Dick, Wuppermann and Company. In 1834 Friedrich returned to Trinidad where he joined his uncles in the firm of Gerold and Urich. He returned to Germany to get married in 1841. In his diary he gives a full description of his proposal to Minchin Bauer:

I went to Minchin's about 11.30. She was sitting at her spinning wheel. "Would you be prepared to share my fate with me? I esteem you very much. That is not enough. I love you very much." In the evening about 7 p.m. I had sherry and a

glass of cider with the Chaplain to give me courage (to talk to her father). "You have a very high
regard for Minchin? Perhaps you have already
come to an understanding? Well, I have no ob-
jections." I leapt down the stairs two at a time -
all my fears, doubts and forebodings vanished and
embracing Minchin, we exchanged our first kiss
- an unforgettable moment, and indeed the most
important day in my life.

Shortly after their marriage, they came
back to Trinidad. In 1855 Friedrich took his family to Australia where his brother-in-law, Bauer,
had a business in Geelong, but after a few years
he returned to Trinidad. In 1860 he separated
from the firm of Gerold and Urich and started his
own commercial business under the name of
F.Urich and Bogen. In 1869 the name became
F.Urich and Son and continued under the management of J.F.Urich until 1890, when it went into
bankruptcy.

Wilhelm Urich, Friedrich's younger
brother, got married in 1845 in Germany and returned to Trinidad with his wife. They lived in
Clarence Street. Their first child, Emma, born on
December 20th 1845, was baptized on 25th January 1846, at Trinity Cathedral. In 1861 the House
of Gerold and Urich passed into the hands of
Wilhelm Urich and his cousin Edward Feez.
Wilhelm retired from business in 1864, and
Wuppermann and Feez became the managing directors of the firm. They took over the Cocal, the
coconut estates at Manzanilla by deed of 19th
October 1866. However, the House of Gerold and

Urich (Wuppermann and Feez) failed on the 21st May 1872. "The failure", (according to the Wuppermann Diary) " was chiefly caused by the Nariva Cocal which had absorbed a capital of $166,000 without being able to pay the current expenses much less the interest on the capital invested. It was Mr Feez's hobby. The house also lost largely in Maturin and other parts of the Main." In 1890 Wilhelm Urich became the owner of the Mayaro Estates.

The Urichs, in short, in nineteenth century Trinidad, carried on extensive business in general merchandize and trade between Trinidad and Venezuela, as well as other commercial undertakings, but it is worthwhile singling out two of their enterprises. They and their associates were largely responsible for the whaling industry in the Gulf of Paria and the production of coconut oil at the Cocal.

Columbus had named the Gulf of Paria, *Golfo de la Ballena*, and in the early nineteenth century, many razor-back whales, up to 80 feet in length, dark on top and pure white underneath, could be seen in the Gulf of Paria, where they came to calf. In 1827 a retired sea Captain from Bermuda, C.A. White, petitioned the Cabildo for permission to open a subscription list to establish a whaling industry. This was granted. Soon there were three whaling stations established, two on Gasparee (one operated by the Tardieus) and one on Monos at present day Copperhole, owned by the Gerolds.

The Gerolds brought down a professional

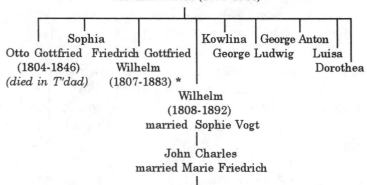

Johann Balthazar Urich (1777-1863)
married
Caroline Gerold (1780-1844)

Sophia   Kowlina George Anton
Otto Gottfried   Friedrich Gottfried   George Ludwig   Luisa
(1804-1846)   Wilhelm   Dorothea
(died in T'dad)   (1807-1883) *

Wilhelm
(1808-1892)
married Sophie Vogt

John Charles
married Marie Friedrich

Paul (1875-1939)
married Marousha (d.1971)
(no issue)

* See page 81 for descendants of Friedrich Gottfried.

GEROLD FAMILY TREE

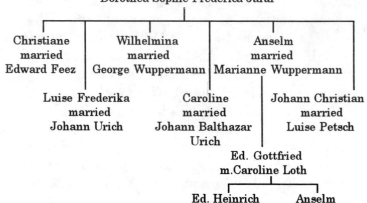

Christian Gottfried Samuel Gerold (1747-1814)
married
Dorothea Sophie Frederica Jafur

Christiane   Wilhelmina   Anselm
married   married   married
Edward Feez   George Wuppermann   Marianne Wuppermann

Luise Frederika   Caroline   Johann Christian
married   married   married
Johann Urich   Johann Balthazar   Luise Petsch
                             Urich

Ed. Gottfried
m.Caroline Loth

Ed. Heinrich   Anselm

harpooner from Germany and in 1834 asked the
Governor Sir George Hill to refuse authorization
for the American Schooner *Harmony*, out of Nan-
tucket, to whale in the Gulf. The German firm
continued the industry till around 1880. The
whales were harpooned and towed into
Copperhole, (then known as Jenny Point, the
Urichs owning 9 acres of land there). Once killed,
the towing of the whale to the station was a te-
dious business and often occupied twenty-four
hours should the wind and tide be against the boat-
men. On arrival, the whale was flensed as near to
the shore as possible and the long slices of blub-
ber carried to the huge sugar coppers, for boiling
to extract the oil, the carnage attracting in an in-
credibly short space of time 1,500 to 3,000 sharks,
so that some of the men had to be employed killing them with harpoons and hatchets. The whales
arrived in December but were then so wild that
they could not be easily approached; the hunting
season was from February to May. The number
of whales caught annually was only twenty-five
to thirty, the oil (about 20,000 gallons) being
brought to Port of Spain for export or local use, as
lamp oil or medicine - whale oil and honey being
supposedly an infallible cure for flu.

The whale hunt (traditionally with a captain at the stern of the pirogue, six stalwart oars-
men and the harpooner in the bow) was described
by Sylvester Devenish in 1871, in enthusiastic
verse, in French, to be sung to the air of Castibelza.

South Quay from the sea, 1850, by Michel Cazabon.
The store of Gerold & Urich opened out onto this Quay.

Whaler in the Second Bocas, by Michel Cazabon.
The whales were larger than the boats which hunted them!

SONG OF THE WHALERS

"Come, quickly launch the pirogue swift,
    The whale is nigh.
The currents, rémou, tidal drift,
    We will defy.
O row, boys row! To storm and sea
    You are no stranger!
Think of the profit - see her flee!
    Forget the danger!"

"The beast is big; much oil there'll be
    For us to share.
Harpoon in hand, I'm right ready,
    The hunt to dare!
So pull, boys, pull! Faster, stronger!
    Don't burn out though,
She won't be below much longer;
    She soon will blow."

Now bounds the boat upon the crest,
    As foam she flings,
And in the trough a moment's rest,
    Then forward springs.
An ebon sheen reflects the light,
    Just near the bow,
It is the whale, most welcome sight.
    "We have her now!"

With sudden spurt near her they bound.
    All tensed, he throws.
The sharp harpoon with whistling sound
    On target goes.
A jet of blood has scarcely spurted
    Into the air,
When instantly, the whale alerted
    Has fled from there.

She plunges to the depths below,
    As Tardieu roars:
"Uncoil the cord and let it go,
    And trail all oars."
Then begins the coursing silent,
    Dragged by the whale,
In the depths, enraged and violent,
    With sweeping tail.

Between two walls of shining foam
    In furrow high,
The canoe glides beneath the dome
    Of silent sky.
And straight to bottom runs the cord
    That's smoking now.
But suddenly the waters roared
    Just near the bow.

The whale, all bloody, surfaced there.
    Without delay,
Approaching her near as they dare,
    Their spirits gay,
With stabs from lances sharp and long
    They kill the beast;
Then fasten her, with joyful song;
    Turn home to feast.

The flag floats proudly at the stern,
    And at this sight,
The few on shore of triumph learn
    With great delight;
And quickly they to others cry,
    And as she nears;
The noble whaler's welcomed by
    A thousand cheers.

In 1874 Charles Kingsley in his book, *At Last a Christmas in the West Indies*, regrets that he missed seeing the processing of a whale.

> On past the whaling quay. It was deserted, for the whales had not yet come in, and there was no chance of seeing a night scene, which is described as horribly beautiful - the sharks around a whale while flensing is going on, each monster bathed in phosphorescent light, which marks his whole outline, and every fin, even his evil eyes and teeth, visible far under water, as the glittering fiend comes up from below, snaps his lump out of the whale's side and is shouldered out of the way by his fellows.

Kingsley also describes, in his inimitable fashion, the coconut works of Gerold and Urich, at Manzanilla.

> All the while the dull thunder of the surf was growing louder and louder, till we rode out upon the shore, and saw before us a right noble sight; a flat, sandy, surf-beaten shore, along which stretched, on one grand curve, lost at last in the haze of spray, fourteen miles of Coco palms.
> At last, after the sun had gone down ... we were aware of lights, and soon found ourselves again in civilization. A large and comfortable house, only just rebuilt after a fire, stood among the palm trees, between the sea and the lagoon; and behind it the barns, sheds and engine houses of the coco-works; and inside it a hearty welcome from a most agreeable German gentleman and his German engineer. A lady's hand - I am sorry to say the lady was not at home - was evident enough in the arrangement of the central room.

Pretty things, a piano, and good books, especially
Longfellow and Tennyson told of cultivation and
taste in that remotest wilderness. We sat up long
into the night around the open door, while the
surf roared, and the palm trees sighed and the
fire-flies twinkled, talking of dear old Germany
and German unity and the possibility of many
things, which have since proved themselves unexpectedly most possible.

We spent the next morning inspecting the works.
We watched the Negros splitting the coco-nuts
with a single blow of that all-useful cutlass, which
they handle with surprising dexterity and force,
throwing the thick husk on one side, the fruit on
the other. We saw the husk carded out by ma-
chinery into its component fibres, for coco-rope
matting, coir rope, saddle stuffing, brushes and
a dozen other uses; while the fruit was crushed
down for the sake of its oil ... all prosperity to the
coco-works of Messrs. Urich and Gerold.

While the members of the French *petite
noblesse* who came to Trinidad, for various reasons creolised rapidly, this was not the case with
the Germans. When Wilhelm (who had married
Sophie Vogt - see family tree on page 71) retired
in 1864, he went to live in Europe - England,
France and Germany - and his son, John Charles
(born in Trinidad in 1849) was educated there. He
had considerable aptitude for music and was a
pupil of Charles François Gounod in London.
Then, living on his income from the Mayaro coconut estates he became a well known amateur com-
poser. His music was at one time used as test
pieces for students, and as a conductor he spent
some time in Moscow. The Port of Spain Gazette

wrote proudly of him in 1879:

A Son of Trinidad.

Mr John Urich, son of William Urich Esq. - His new Opera Comique "L'Orage" was performed for the first time at the Theatre Royal de la Monnaie of Brussels. At the fall of the curtain, Mr Urich was loudly called for and vociferously cheered by the audience. The libreto is a sweet and touching idyll of pastoral love by Mr Armand Sylvestre.

Urich's later operas included the following: Le Serment (Brussels, 1883); Flora Macdonald (Bologna, 1885); Le Pilote (Monte Carlo, 1889); Le Carillon (Aix-les-Bains, 1895); Herman and Dorothea (Berlin, 1899); The Cicada (London, 1912); Ariane (not produced, overture performed in Paris, 1904); Tsing-Tau (London, 1914).

John married Marie Friedrich. He stayed in Europe for the rest of his long life and died in 1939, aged ninety. His son Paul, born in 1875, married a White Russian (now known as Bellorussian) and they lived in Moscow for seven years. Marousha, Paul's wife, was from a family of thirteen and full of energy. Paul came out to Trinidad about 1900, to run the family coconut estates at Mayaro. For some unknown reason (though Trinidad macomehs supplied many) Marousha arrived out several months later than Paul, able to speak only one word of English and quite penniless. She simply kept repeating "Paul Urich wife" and eventually one of his acquaintances took her to far off Mayaro. Paul was made a justice of the Peace for the district, and his estates,

Lagon Doux, St. Bernard, Perseverance and La Cordonière flourished. When he died, he left Marousha a rich woman and still unable to speak English properly, though fluent in French. She was a capable businesswoman and had a kind heart, donating the money to establish 'Nichol's Nursing Home', on condition that she was cared for there when she was ill. She died in 1971.

Otto Gottfried was the oldest of Johann Balthazar Urich's sons. His brother Friedrich had sent him regularly from Trinidad extracts from his diary (1830-1832) which absolutely fascinated the older brother. Finally, when he had graduated as a doctor in Germany, in 1837, Otto took the plunge and came out to practice medicine in Trinidad. Unfortunately, he died after just a few years in the island. He was buried in Lapeyrouse cemetery and his grave was adorned with a large bronze medallion, designed and made by the famous Venezuelan sculptor, Palacio. This was, however, stolen in 1907.

Friedrich, the first Urich to come to Trinidad, had married Wilhelmina Bauer in Germany. He had three sons, (see family tree page 81) and one daughter, Sophie, all born in Trinidad. The family lived at Abercromby Street. Their first child Johann Frederick, born on the 4th July 1842, was Baptized at Trinity Cathedral on the 7th October. When he was twenty-seven years old, he married Marie Kernahan in St Thomas in 1869. Carl, Friedrich's second son, married Maria Affanador, their son José Fritz settling with his wife (née Caranza) and family in Venezuela; Adolf

Christian, the youngest son, did a Doctorate in
Philosophy and Chemistry at Heidelberg University. On his return to Trinidad, he wed Maie
Kernahan, the twin sister of Marie. For a number
of years Adolph Urich Ph.D. was the Secretary-
Treasurer of the Scientific Association of Trinidad,
founded in 1863 'For the cultivation of Scientific
knowledge in the West Indies', and which gave way
in the early 1890's to the Field Naturalist Society.

Adolf kept up his German connections. His
daughter Irene was crippled by infantile paraly-
sis (polio) and he took her to Germany for correc-
tive surgery when she was age twelve. She remained there a number of years, acquiring a fluent knowledge of German. The surgery was quite
successful and enabled her to walk around with
the aid of a walking stick. Irene was a very coura-
geous woman and undertook the difficult task of
deciphering and translating her grandfather's diary from the German, as well as caring for her ill
sister. Adolph's son, Leo Wilfred Gottfried Urich,
was born in Trinidad in 1899, and attended
Queen's Royal College in Port of Spain, then did a
Medical degree at London University, specializ-
ing in Tropical Medicine. He served in the Colonial Hospital in Port of Spain, was made Medical
Superintendent of the Leper asylum in
Chacachacare and acted as Director of Medical
Services in Trinidad. His two children, at present
live in England.

The Kernahan sisters were staunch Catholics (Irish creoles whose grandfather had been a
protestant and had married a French creole Catho-

lic) and in getting married to them, the Urich
brothers had promised to allow the children to be
brought up as Catholics. Frederick was in general quite tolerant of his wife's religion, but there
were occasions when on a Sunday morning he deliberately kept the doors of the house locked, and
his wife and children had to climb out the window
in order to go to Mass. Marie made sure that her
children got a good Catholic education even from
primary school. Otto, for instance, went to a private school run by Mrs. Gawthorne on the Almond
Walk (Broadway). She wrote of him: 'Otto Urich
used to get as excited over Sacred History as if
what was read was taking place before him. When
Joseph wanted to keep back Benjamin (in Egypt)
he bawled out: "Let him go, the old man is waiting
for him".' But the boy's faith was quite shaken
when the priest hearing confessions in the Cathedral ran out of the confessional as a huge blue crab
(escaped from a *marchande* nearby) approached
him, - no doubt, in view of its impending death,
wishing to be absolved from its sins! Otto said he
could never like the priest again - "A man afraid
of a crab!"

The boys had their secondary schooling at
St Mary's College and the girls at St Joseph's convent. Frederick's children married into 'French'
creole, Catholic families - by 1910, the French creole society had expanded to include Corsican, Irish,
English and German on an equal basis with the
French, as long as they were Catholics. Before
the start of the First World War, German creoles
had married into almost all the leading French

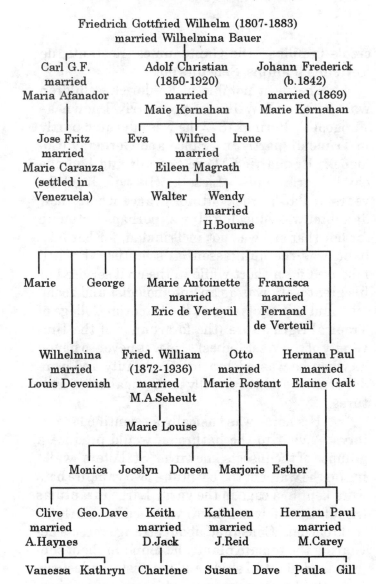

Friedrich Gottfried Wilhelm (1807-1883)
married Wilhelmina Bauer

Carl G.F.
married
Maria Afanador

Adolf Christian
(1850-1920)
married
Maie Kernahan

Johann Frederick
(b.1842)
married (1869)
Marie Kernahan

Jose Fritz
married
Marie Caranza
(settled in
Venezuela)

Eva   Wilfred   Irene
married
Eileen Magrath

Walter   Wendy
married
H.Bourne

Marie   George   Marie Antoinette
married
Eric de Verteuil

Francisca
married
Fernand
de Verteuil

Wilhelmina
married
Louis Devenish

Fried. William
(1872-1936)
married
M.A.Seheult

Otto
married
Marie Rostant

Herman Paul
married
Elaine Galt

Marie Louise

Monica   Jocelyn   Doreen   Marjorie   Esther

Clive   Geo.Dave
married
A.Haynes

Keith
married
D.Jack

Kathleen
married
J.Reid

Herman Paul
married
M.Carey

Vanessa   Kathryn   Charlene   Susan   Dave   Paula   Gill creole families - the Ganteaumes, Rostants, de Verteuils, Pantins, Seheults etc.

The most notable of Frederick's children was Friedrick William, popularly known as 'Jangoons'. Born in 1872, he was educated partly in Trinidad, partly in France and Germany (Cologne). He married Marie Seheult and had one child, Marie Louise (Liesel). His wife lived for years at Pau in the south of France where their daughter was educated. It was perhaps fortunate for her that she was not in Trinidad, for her husband was the quintessential scientist. He had laboured for a short while in the civil service but his great work was as an entomologist and zoologist, and as a professor at the Imperial College of Tropical Agriculture (the forerunner of the University of the West Indies). He was never so happy as when he was celebrating the beauty and wonder of nature and especially in the smallest of creatures.

His home was basically a scientific laboratory. A visit to the bathroom would produce a glimpse of the insects known as "St. Peters" walking on the water of the bathtub. Two vampire bats were kept in a cage in the yard. Large tarantulas (hopefully safely confined) were fed regularly on cockroaches. Consulted about strange insects devouring the tomato plants, he found in them subjects for delightful study and not pests for destruction. But his favourite pet, which was often given the run of the yard, was a thick, six-foot-long macajuel, named Cleo. On one occasion while he was entertaining guests, most appalling screams were heard coming from the maid in the yard. Urich rushed out and returned in a moment to the house, quite calmly announcing *en passant* that it was only Cleo - the maid had gone to the dimly lit toilet and once *in situ* had discovered to her shock that Cleo was inspecting her from close proximity.

Urich was a most congenial companion. In *Snake Hunter's Holiday*, by Ditmars and Bridges, a description is given of him and his house in 1930:

> About ten o'clock we called on the professor. He lived behind a pink stucco wall and an iron grill gate in a tiny little house that looked old-fashioned even for Port of Spain, where gingerbread effects are much appreciated as additions to architecture. We knocked and waited, knocked again and waited again, and presently an ancient Negress opened the door a crack and peered out. She promised to see if the professor was at home and we stood in the sun and mopped our faces until she returned and silently opened the door. Cécilia was a master of English and *patois* and as deft at mixing rum punch as her master, we discovered later, but she never used words when a gesture would talk for her.
>
> One glance around the living-room told us we had not mistaken the house - a naturalist lived here. Professor Urich's living room spoke eloquently of a man and a scientist. There were a couple of small tables, marble-topped and unadorned, a few chairs, some stiff old oil paintings of stiff old gentlemen (his ancestors), and that was all that really belonged to the room. Everything else was there because the professor had dropped it there when he came in from a field

excursion. A bay window was pretty well taken up with empty cages of wire and wood; you had to look smart or you would trip over cans for transporting small fish. A heap of collecting bags filled one corner, bat nets held the place of honour in the only rocking chair, and the handles leaned against the wall. The place was clean - scrubbed and spotless - but it was the habitation of a man who lived alone and for his own convenience.

By all accounts, Professor Urich knew more about the natural history of Trinidad than any man living.... He was stout and grizzled with a heavy, furrowed face tanned by many an expedition afield. But his face was kindly and stamped with that thoughtfulness and openness that you so often find in men who have spent their lives working out the puzzles of nature.....

We returned to Port of Spain and the professor took up the familiar shouting, "Cécilia, fais trey punch!". "You know, your President, Teddy Roosevelt, was fond of rum punch," he remarked as we sat around the little marble-topped table in his living room in the fast-gathering darkness, "He visited me here in 1916. At that time I happened to be in South Trinidad working on cane parasites and a messenger came out with orders to return to Port of Spain immediately. Teddy wanted to see the natural history of the island and I was assigned to show it to him. I think I must have succeeded. I showed him everything". "I rather think he was on a diet of some kind then and Mrs Roosevelt didn't want him to drink, but we used to stop in here before we reported to his hotel after a day in the field, and have two or three rounds of rum punch. The day we went to the bat cave, he told me to bring along a flask of punch. He told Mrs Roosevelt it was cold tea.

Oh yes, Teddy was dee-lighted with the punch".

Urich was a foundation member (along with Broadway, Caracciolo and Mole) of the Field Naturalist Society, which held their first meeting on the 10th July 1891. He was for some time the Secretary-Treasurer and contributed numerous papers to the society, being an active member till shortly before his death. His papers were always interesting, for instance, speaking on "Mosquitoes and how to deal with them", not alone did he suggest using the tiny fish *Cyprinodonte* to control the larvae, but he brought a bowl of the fish into which he poured the larvae, which the fish (presumably starved in advance!) hungrily devoured. He stated that though a $100 prize had been offered for the best means of raising dragonflies to eat mosquitoes, there were as yet no practical results. He ended by recommending that Eucalyptus branches could be hung by windows, the smell driving the mosquitoes away. Speaking on the feeding habits and skin-shedding of the rattle snake, he brought a snake to the proceedings - but the animal would not oblige, it neither ate nor shed its skin nor rattled.

The following are extracts from the September 1937 issue of the "Tropical Agriculture Journal," published shortly after Jangoon's death.

Urich was a particularly outstanding example of the "born naturalist", a type which is all too rare in these days. He was one of those students to whom scientific observation of living things is second nature and in his own subject, he certainly had an infinite capacity for taking pains. No group of animals ever seems to have been too insignificant to attract his attention with the result that his knowledge of species and of their modes of life was monumental.

A lifetime of distinguished technical work can hardly be summarised, but among the many problems which he studied may be mentioned his work on the Cacao Thrips and on the Sugar-Cane Froghopper. His work on the former pest attracted much attention and he spent some time in the neighbouring colonies giving advice on control measures and even travelled to San Thomé at the instance of the Portuguese Government. He was also one of the very first entomologists to recognise the possibilities of the biological control of insect pests and he did much to put this on a scientific basis. Several outstandingly successful introductions of predacious and parasitic insects into other countries from Trinidad are the direct outcome of his pioneer work in this field.

As a field naturalist Urich was unsurpassed. His knowledge of the local fauna was truly amazing and he has done much to encourage its study by others, being a foundation member of the Field Naturalists' Club and an active participant in its functions to the end of his life. His reputation abroad was, indeed as much due to his work as a naturalist as to his more strictly official achievements, a reputation which his considerable linguistic ability did much to assist.

But apart from his technical qualifications, Urich will long be remembered for his engaging personality. He was a man of simple, yet cultivated tastes in many ways and he had the gift of making and retaining friendships. Several generations of students from the Imperial College will have kindly recollections of his association. Naturally, we who worked in his own department knew him best, but for several years he came into contact with members of other departments, particularly through the week-end excursions which he used to organise to Aripo, Tuchuche and other parts of the Northern Range, of which he was so fond.

His services were retained for the study of the local bats, in connection with the campaign against paralytic rabies. In this subject he made some notable discoveries on the feeding habits of the carnivorous bats, which have a great importance in control operations. It is fortunate that he was able to publish at least a part of his work on this subject before his illness overtook him.

The importance of Urich's contribution to the scientific world becomes clear when account is taken of the numerous new animal species that he discovered in Trinidad, which were hitherto unknown to modern science and which consequently have been named after him. The distribution of few (if any) is confined to Trinidad, and subsequent to his identification of the species, most have been discovered also on the South American mainland. Not surprisingly since Urich was primarily an entomologist, sixteen species of insects are numbered among the new species: five types of ants, a moth, a butterfly and nine other kinds of insects, including *Liothrips urichi*, which was used in one of the earliest examples of biological control. But in accord with the scientist's wide range of interests, discoveries named after him vary widely, from a tiny field mouse, *Akodon urichi*, to a cute little frog with iridescent blue eyes,

Eleutherodactylus urichi and even to a plant, a vine of the family *Vacciniaceae* with wax-like red and white flowers, *Psammisia urichi*, (common name, wild clove) found only at the top of Mount Tucuche and Cerro del Aripo. A complete list of his discoveries is given in the notes at the back of the book.

Even when he was well past middle age "Jangoons" continued to lead expeditions to the northern range. One of his friends describes a visit to look for Guacharo birds:

As I grew up our friendship became closer because of photography. He had very good equipment and often worked late into the night. I was always there with him. I became a very good photographer myself. He used to lend me his valuable equipment when I went off for jaunts into the country. We had many expeditions together. One of the most interesting was a visit to the caves in the Oropouche valley. We left before dawn and met the other members of the party at the end of the driving road about nine miles from the caves. There were about ten of us in the party, which included Sir Geoffrey Evans, the Principal of I.C.T.A. and a few students. The walk, up hill and down dale for 9 miles was strenuous. We each carried a torch and our food. Among mine was a thermos of hot coffee. The cave follows the course of a subterranean river. It was not easy going in pitch darkness. At times the roof was very low. There was danger of hitting your head on the stalactites. Before each step one had to ascertain the height of the roof above and the depth of the stream below. The only sounds were the murmur of the stream and the flapping of the wings of the wachero birds, that are the size of a chicken. Sometimes one had to clamber over rocks that were very slippery with the droppings of the birds. In some places the stream was broad and shallow, in others it was narrow and deep. We were sometimes up to our waists in water. There was always the danger of dropping our torches which would have put us in a very difficult position. We travelled about a mile up the caves. No one has ever been to the end of it. There is a deep cave at the top of the Aripo Range which is supposed to be the source of the stream but no one has ever entered one end and come out at the other. My hot coffee came in very useful on the way back. Jangoons, who was getting old then, looked very tired. He had to have a rest. I gave him my hot coffee. Got him to sit on a log and told the others to carry on. I would come along very slowly with Jangoons. We managed to get back to the car before dark. I cannot close this part of my recollections without mentioning Jangoons' rum punches. They were famous. It was a ritual with him. The most important part was a fresh lime preferably just picked off the tree. The punch was not mixed in a jug like everybody else's. That No! The glasses were placed in a row. Into each was placed a small quantity of sugar. Then a little water to melt the sugar, then the rum (and lime) and last of all crushed ice to fill the glass. Each was mixed with a small spoon and then ready to be consumed.

George Adolph, Friedrick William's eldest brother, and Marie, his eldest sister never married. George Adolph, born in 1874, was educated at St Mary's College and at Bingen and

Darmstadt, in Germany. He was in the island's
Civil Service. Marie suffered from Polio and was
sent to Germany for electrical treatment. Her 'diary' of the stay in Germany makes interesting
reading.

Wilhelmina (another sister) married Louis
Devenish and bore him six children: Ivan, Kevin,
Everard, Joan, Herwald and Harold. Her two
younger sisters, Francisca and Marie Antoinette,
had a double wedding with two doctors, the de
Verteuil brothers Fernand and Eric. Otto, a
younger brother, was manager of Andrew
Kernahan's coconut estates at Cedros, San
Quentin, Les Pomier and Garden.   The
neighbouring estates owned by the Colonial Company were managed by Louis Rostant who had two
beautiful daughters. Not surprisingly, on 23rd
October 1913, Otto married Marie Rostant, the
second daughter, at the Church of the Holy Rosary in Port of Spain. Otto died within a few years
of the marriage and his wife shortly after, leaving
five daughters. Jocelyn, the second oldest, joined
the Sisters of St Joseph of Cluny, was the Principal of St Joseph's Convent San Fernando 1957-
1965, the Principal of St Joseph's Convent, Port
of Spain, 1954-1957 and 1965-73 and Provincial
Superior of the St Joseph of Cluny Sisters in
Trinidad & Tobago, St Lucia, St Vincent and
Grenada from 1963-1980, being the first
Trinidadian to hold these posts.

Herman Paul, the youngest of Frederick's
sons, was the only one to go into business - (George
had been in the civil service) - becoming eventu-

Paul Urich on the beach at Point Radix.
The St. Bernard coconut estate is in the shadow of the Point.

Schweizer House, the Urich's residence in St. Anns, built 1888.
Irene Urich with Gottfried and Yvonne de Verteuil.

A double wedding, two Urich sisters and two de Verteuil brothers, 1910.
From left: Dr. Eric de Verteuil & Marie Antoinette Urich, Dr. Fernand de Verteuil and Francisca Urich. Fernand's progeny were to be: Gottfried, Yvonne and Fernand; and Eric's: Ulric, Elissa, Maureen, Ian, Eric, Anthony.

Jangoon's Urich and his brother Otto, (with hat), at Cedros, having a drink before lunch.

Otto Urich's five daughter's (1990).

Marjorie   Monica   Doreen   Jocelyn   Esther
Mrs Collier   Mrs Hamel-Smith   Mrs Bromage   Sr.Francis Xavier   Mrs Dalgliesh

Above:
The Doctor's House Chacachacare, home of Dr. Wilfred Urich.
Below:
His children, Walter & Wendy, with Jean & Marie Anne
Wuppermann, and their ever-faithful 'nanny,' Dorothy Clarke.

ally the Manager of the Royal Bank of Canada, in
Port of Spain. He married Elaine Galt and had
five children. (See family tree on page 81). George
Dave became a fighter pilot in the Second World
War and was killed in action, Keith was in business and Clive became an agriculturalist; following in the footsteps of his uncle he possesses a
magnificent butterfly collection and indeed, breeds
butterflies to export the chrysalises to Kew Gardens England for hatching. Herman Paul Jnr.,
Trinidad's first Junior Lawn Tennis Champion,
followed almost exactly in his father's footsteps,
as a banker. His son Dave will possibly, in a few
years time, be the only one to bear the name Urich
in Trinidad and to prevent it fading into the shad-
ows of the past.

Chapter 3

The Stollmeyer Family

Thus grave these lessons on thy soul -
Hope, faith and love; and thou shalt find
Strength when life's surges rudest roll,
Light when thou else wert blind!
                    Johann Christoph Friedrich Von Schiller.

An American millionaire giving a talk to the youths of his town told them: "When I first came here fifty years ago all I had with me was a few possessions wrapped in a handkerchief". Though most of the audience were duly impressed, one young man asked: "Please Sir, tell us what you had wrapped in your handkerchief". The embarrassed lecturer replied: "Fifty thousand dollars in blue chip bonds". When Conrad Frederick Stollmeyer came to Trinidad in 1845, he landed with $5 in his pocket. Fifty years later he was a millionaire; the wealth he brought with him was his resilient character.

The Stollmeyer family in the late middle ages lived in Venice. From Venice they came to the town of Ulm, on the Danube. (See map on page 35). From the 11th century Ulm had been an Imperial Free City, at one time ruling over a district of 300 square miles; but in 1803 it became part of Bavaria, and a few years later it was incorporated into the Duchy of Wurttemberg.

Conrad Frederick Stollmeyer was born in 1813 in
Ulm, his parents belonging to the patrician families of the ancient free city. It was at Ulm, in October 1805, that the Austrian General, Mack, with
an army of 23,000 men, capitulated to Napoleon.
Perhaps, Conrad inherited his disgust with Bavaria and hatred for war from the older members
of his family who had passed through these expe-
riences. Certain it is, that after working his way
through secondary school and (at age eighteen)
going to the University of Stotsigen, he steadfastly
set himself against serving in the army of the King
of Wurttemberg and he used to relate many years
later with great gusto, how a few days before the
time for his conscription to the army, he ascertained who was the army surgeon responsible for
the passing of the recruits; how he called upon him
and asked him to examine him and paying him a
handsome fee told him that he was afflicted with
"great shortness of breath when he ran up a hill".
When the day came for him to go before the board
of officers the doctor rejected him as having a short
neck. The astonishment of his comrades was great
when he told them "What", they exclaimed, "you
the best runner, the best fencer (he was ambidextrous) the best pistol shot we have among us."
"Yes" he said "they say I am not fit to be a sol-
dier".

   At the University he could not stand the
beer-drinking bouts so typical of German University students, and acquired a lasting aversion to
alcohol. He also acquired Theistic ideas, probably
from the philosophy of Spinoza through Schiller,

and Goethe's teaching of material evolution. Like
all Theists, Conrad believed in the immanence of
God, that God was somehow part of the world, that
the human soul was evolving and to be reincar-
nated, and because of these beliefs he struggled
throughout his life with the problem of evil in this
world.

After leaving University, Conrad spent a
year at Mayence in the office of a hotel, and in
1836, at the age of 23, emigrated to the United
States of America. He was to write later from
Trinidad:

> Bavaria is old and overpopulated and the life of a
> lowly Royal Bavarian Civil Servant is such a
> miserable one..... If I had remained in Germany,
> without a doubt I would have mixed up in poli-
> tics and would either have been shot, put to the
> gallows or put in prison for the duration of my
> life.... As a boy of fourteen I had to go through a
> hard apprenticeship far from home. My first job
> was to serve drunken students. Rarely did I visit
> the house of my parents to rest from my labours.
> It should be easily understood that such condi-
> tions made me leave, to go as far as possible. My
> ideas and my memories of Ulm or Germany were
> never inviting. Here I have made a new home.
> My land is large....

In the United States, he settled in the town
of Philadelphia, where many of his fellow Germans
were domiciled. There he became a printer and
married Anna Snyder, of German descent. He
interested himself in designing a type-setting
machine - but the compositors at the firm were so

fearful of losing their jobs, they flung the pieces of
type-metal at his head. A born businessman, he
founded a German Settlement Company to obtain
land for German immigrants, and became a citizen of the United States. He was a committee
member of the anti-slavery Society in Pennsylva-
nia and along with another German, Kidderlin,
he edited in Philadelphia a German-language
newspaper which strongly advocated the freedom
of the slaves in the southern United States. He
threw himself heart and soul into the anti-slavery
campaign and on one occasion, in a leader he was
afterwards fond of quoting, he aroused the fury of
the pro-slavery party by rebuking them with the
words of the American Declaration of Independence which pronounced all men to be born free
and equal, while the nation held some two million
black people in slavery. The result was that the
opposition paper declared that Stollmeyer should
be hanged on one side of the church and the
Lutheran parson should meet with a similar fate
on the other. His printing office was subsequently
wrecked and he had to flee for his life.

In his printery Stollmeyer had also published tracts for a fellow German named J. A. Etzler
who was trying to muster adherents to form a community in which all the drudgery would be performed by machines, leaving the community free
to devote themselves to a life of leisure and the
pursuit of the arts. But apparently the scheme
was not sufficiently hare-brained to attract any
Americans; and so, sometime in the early 1840's
after spending nearly seven years in the States,

Etzler and Stollmeyer (with his wife and three children) emigrated to England.

There, they were engaged at first in attempting to use wave power as a motive force for vessels, Stollmeyer exhausting his meagre funds in this experiment. But with all the new scientific discoveries and especially the success of the railway, the times were propitious for new ventures, and the two Germans had ambitious and extraordinary ideas. In October 1844 they formed *The Tropical Emigration Society*, with Etzler as President and Stollmeyer as Secretary. They went lecturing in the cold, grimy industrial towns of northern England, recruiting volunteers by spinning fantastic stories, which apparently they themselves believed: "the beautiful, ever-mild, and evergreen tropical countries where 1 acre bananas produces as much nutritive stuff as 133 acres wheat or 44 acres potatoes". The Venezuelan Government granted Etzler 200 acres at Guinamita, on the Gulf of Paria, four hours by boat from Trinidad; and this gave the pair of adventurers the opportunity of being engineer and consultant for another company. This was *The Trinidad Great Eastern and South Western Railway Company*, which proposed to build a railway, on rails of wood, 'from Port of Spain to the principal port, Port Royal' - (apparently the directors of the Company by *Port Royal* meant Chaguaramus, and the railway would have gone from there to Mayaro). In February 1845 Stollmeyer founded a third company, *The Venezuelan Transit Company*, which would provide transport for the hundreds or thousands of settlers wishing to join the community in the tropics.

Etzler and Stollmeyer came to Trinidad in December 1845. A few of the two or three hundred emigrants who arrived actually reached Venezuela, where numbers died of malaria and yellow fever and were rescued by an expedition from Trinidad. Most then emigrated to the United States and elsewhere or returned to England, though a few settled in Trinidad (which was apparently part of the original plan) and their descendants still live here - names like Tomlinson, Carr, Palmer, Rapsey, Tucker come to mind. Etzler disappeared, and Stollmeyer settled in Trinidad, - without employ since the bubble Railway company had burst.

Friends were kind to the penniless young German and his family, and most importantly of all he won the friendship of the Governor, Lord Harris. Lord Harris, finding him an interesting man to converse with, actually gave him a horse so that they could both ride out together to talk over many things. Through the Governor's kindness he obtained the job of doing all the laundry work of the regiment of soldiers then stationed at St James Barracks; also the supplying of firewood to that same institution and others. He borrowed some money as working capital and within a month was able to pay it back. The firewood was cut at Cocorite which was then in a state of high woods or swamp; and as the land was cleared Stollmeyer planted coconut trees. When these came into bearing, he being a strict total abstainer, and hoping that the people in Port of Spain might be induced to drink less rum which in those days was only 10 cents a bottle, sent out water coconuts in donkey carts - and he always boasted afterwards that he was the one who started the coconut-water trade in the capital. The trade helped to support his family, but unfortunately for his idea of promoting temperance, the cute citizens of Port of Spain soon discovered that coconut water could be improved by the addition of alcohol!

During 1849, whilst still carrying on the clearing and cultivation of coconuts on the land at Cocorite, Stollmeyer somehow became interested in asphalt, or pitch as it was then called, and he took a trip to La Brea. While there he came in contact with Thomas Cochrane, the 10th Earl of Dundonald, who commanded the Royal Navy's American and West Indian Station from 1848-1851. The Earl owned one or two small parcels of land in the village of La Brea and he was on the point of acquiring from Government a lease on a portion of the Pitch Lake. The Earl was anxious to find someone to work his lands with a view to the shipment of asphalt to Europe, and on the recommendation of Lord Harris he approached Stollmeyer who was only too ready to undertake the task. This, the energetic German carried on for some years to the mutual benefit of the Earl and himself.

Stollmeyer was also contracted by Lord Harris to lay a water supply from the Maraval River for Port of Spain. The temperance advocate always boasted that it was he who first suggested (successfully) to the Governor that to provide the funds for the scheme, an excise tax should be placed on rum. The waterworks were completed shortly after the departure of Lord Harris from the island. At this period too, the German immigrant was involved in a newspaper or periodical called *The Trinidadian* which was published from 1846-1853. Supposedly he was editor for a number of years.

By 1853 Conrad had saved enough money to acquire Merrimac Estate, about a quarter-mile from the Pitch Lake, and also Lever Estate. Not satisfied with Merrimac estate as only an agricultural property, he started a brick factory there. Though the work at Cocorite was given up and the land leased out at a small rental, and his main work was at La Brea, Stollmeyer elected to make Port of Spain his main domicile and only went periodically to spend time in La Brea. But in 1854 disaster nearly struck. For two months Cholera ravaged Trinidad and particularly Port of Spain. Carts rumbled through the deserted streets carrying their grim load of coffins. People died so fast that they were buried in hurriedly dug trenches at Lapeyrouse cemetery in unmarked graves. It was with many, a case of 'well in the morning, dead by night'. Some who were sick for only three or four hours died of dehydration. The medicine usually employed and considered the most successful was diluted sulphuric acid and iced water. Conrad Stollmeyer had a very bad attack of Cholera; for two days he lay extremely sick in bed and rumours of his death made the rounds in

town.   But he recovered fully, though he had to
spend another two days flat in bed. His wife was
ill for nine crucial hours, but cheated death. Nearly
half the people of the town were stricken and one
in five died. Once he was up on his feet, Stollmeyer
brought pitch to town and this he burned at every
street corner to purify the air. The chief medical
officer of health declared that had it not been for
this enterprising and public-spirited German
things would have been far worse. How far modern medicine would agree with this verdict is, to
say the least, doubtful.

In 1854 he wrote his mother:

> I own my land outright, none of my property is
> mortgaged. My cash (gold) is sufficient to run
> my business to advantage. In my business with
> scrap metal (iron, copper, lead etc) I can make at
> least 25% profit after deduction of all expenses.
> At present my brick factory at La Brea promises
> to be the surest source of profit. I employ 30
> labourers and have orders for more bricks than I
> can manufacture. The whole factory is mine....
> The former conditions under slavery have spoilt
> the labourers here and they hate to work. A negro
> can live on very, very little, and works only when
> he has no money, or when he wants to drink rum.
> Naturally there are exceptions. To have the work
> done of about 30 labourers, one has to engage 40.

In 1855 everything was still going wonderfully for him:

> Paradise must have been in a tropical climate
> and the Elysian fields of the philosophers would

have destroyed the idea of winter. Here the
people work as little as possible, just enough work
to make a bare living. All stores, shops and business houses close at 4 p.m. and then all merchants
and clerks ride horses or in carriages or take a
walk. The final weeks of the year are used for
races, and an exhibition of flowers, fruits and
provisions. All stores are closed at 12 p.m. during these weeks. I received the large silver medal
for asphalt and this year again the same medal
for my bricks etc. Generally speaking I have every reason to be satisfied with the progress of my
various industries. I have always so many irons
in the fire that even if one or the other is burnt
the rest will cover the damage.

The young German had such an active and
inventive mind that it gave him no rest. Passing
through the swamps in the south of Trinidad and
glimpsing the enormous stands of the ten-foot
high, swamp aroid *Montrichardia Aculiata* (sometimes considered a variety of *Montrichardia
Aborescens*) he immediately named it "the
Trinidad Paper Plant"; and then sent 40 bundles
of it through Irving, Elsworth and Holmes to the
Editor and Proprietor of the Times, for the purpose of having practical trials made by their paper manufacturers. Regrettably, eight months
later he got the news that 'the fibre will not take'.
That same year large stands of Mora,
Balata, Watercare and Cedar were discovered in
the Irois area in the south of Trinidad, within the
Gulf of Paria, where vessels could lay safe and
convenient to take on the timber. The Colonial
Government undertook to procure the timber, with

the labour of prisoners in the forest, and then to saw it up by means of a steam saw-mill in Port of Spain, for use in building the Hospital, the Lunatic Asylum and a bridge over the Caroni. Stollmeyer got the contract for the transport of the timber, bought two sailing ships, hired a third and constructed rafts for the transport of the timber. Seeing all the available hardwood, his mind once more reverted to the construction of a railway but he failed to get either private funding or Government support. However William Eccles, one of the most wealthy sugar planters showed great interest. To facilitate transport of his sugar, the planter cut a light railway track (the Cipero Tramway) through a hill and connected San Fernando with the Creek, and at Cipero Creek he erected cranes for loading and unloading ships and a warehouse for sugar. Stollmeyer dug 3,000 tons of pitch from the Lake to supply Eccles in order to construct the tow-path for the mules to pull the railway wagons.

It was shortly after this time, that Stollmeyer began to export greater quantities of pitch to Europe, probably in conjunction with the Earl of Dundonald (or possibly his good friend, the wealthy Corsican, Andre Blasini); in 1856, 240 tons were shipped to France; in 1857, he 'disposed of a great quantity of asphalt'. For the remainder of his life, asphalt from the pitch lake was to be the great source of his revenue. He devoted a great deal of time and energy to this project which had very many ups and downs. His correspondence on the Pitch Lake and export of asphalt which has come down to us, fills three volumes.

In 1857 Conrad bought the property at the corner of Richmond and London Streets. In November 1857 he wrote to his mother:

"On July 21st, I bought one of the finest and most beautiful houses in Port of Spain. After I have spent perhaps $1,000 on painters, paper hangers and carpenters, it is in such a condition that no other expenses will be necessary for the next ten years. We moved in at the end of September. The location of the house is almost at the centre of the city and very near to the Government buildings. It has a garden with columns and fruit trees and a stone wall around it. The land and the house form a corner of two streets. It is 208 feet long on one side, the other measures 118 feet. It forms a parallelogram and is almost one and a half acres. Today I could get $1,000 more than I paid for the house, land and all expenses, but I haven't the slightest idea to sell. We may as well live in a beautiful house as the other people who want to acquire it now, perhaps better we, as being water drinkers and of a very simple living standard, we spend much less than those who have the same means.

I had a mind to move to La Brea, but as my business activities make it necessary that I am in Port of Spain, and as I have bought the house in Port of Spain, I changed my plans. I will always make Port of Spain my main domicile.

We have to be grateful to God for everything we have. Dissatisfaction with our possessions, as long as there exists no real need, is ingratitude towards God.

In 1858 Stollmeyer began to distill oil from

the pitch lake for use in lamps, to produce what we would now call kerosene. In that year he wrote proudly:

> Trinidad burning oil is now used in all the principal houses here. I use no other oil in my house. I have four lamps; one large and very handsome which cost me $7, and three smaller lamps which sell at $4 each. These lamps were imported by Mr Philbrick, and I believe gave him a handsome profit. The burning oil sells at $1.25 per English Imperial Gallon. As the asphalt oil gives a better light than coconut oil, it is cheaper at equal prices per gallon. You are probably aware that common lamps will not answer for the asphalt oil.

The 11th Earl of Dundonald in the early 1860's formed his father's holdings of pitch into a company, not only to mine and export asphalt but also to distill oil from the asphalt - following Stollmeyer's process; but the Company failed within 18 months due to the discovery and processing of petroleum in the States and its export at a very low price as lamp oil. One legacy of Conrad's venture, however, is that in Trinidad kerosene is still known as pitch-oil.

The young German was so resilient that the impression is sometimes given that he went from success to success. This is not at all the case. His letters list all sorts of disasters: 'A couple of negroes left without saying goodbye and I lost a couple of hundred dollars'; 'My boat was destroyed through arson - lost $1,500; an accident with the other boat cost $600'; 'I have suffered losses which made me

Conrad Frederick Stollmeyer by Michel Cazabon.
Cazabon catches the look of an eccentric genius.

Conrad's wife, Anna, née Snyder, by Michel Cazabon.
The strength of her character is evident.

Conrad's son, Charles Fourier,
in typical turn-of-the-century elegance.

A sketch by Gerald G. Watterson.
Stollmeyer's House at the corner of Richmond & London Streets.
Bought in 1857, it was "one of the finest houses in town".

ask several times, "why me?"' But his philosophy
of life enabled him to face up to everything.

> What ever happens to us in our life has its own
> meaning, either it is the consequence of former
> mistakes or it is the proving stone needed to
> improve our character. I do remember that when
> I was in University, professor Baumer said: A
> genuine diamond is of more value when cut and
> polished on all sides. The procedure of grinding
> and polishing of course is not a very pleasant
> matter, but seems to be as necessary for the re-
> sult, as it is useful later on. The longest life is
> probably the one which has the most experiences.
> A person who never had bad times does not know
> the value of happiness, tranquillity and content-
> ment and resembles more a statue than a hu-
> man being.
> The person who does not lose his dignity in time
> of adversity, puts his trust in God, and voluntar-
> ily sacrifices everything, (particularly the outer
> appearances of imagined wealth which are use-
> less and harmful) stands much higher, and has a
> higher estimation in the eyes of all right-think-
> ing people.
> More than once, it was the case that I had to say
> to myself, 'you lost everything but honour, con-
> science, hope and energy to start again.' I am
> not sorry for my past life. I gained experiences
> which are worth more than they have cost me.

Stollmeyer was later to continue his venture in asphalt with a businessman called
Finlayson, but meanwhile in 1868 the Government
appointed him to be superintendent of a convict
station at Irois. Convicts were there to be pun-

ished by hard work and to be rehabilitated through
agriculture. They planted food like vegetables and
peas, which when reaped were sent to Port of Spain
by lighter to distribute to the different institutions.
Stollmeyer who was fascinated by the coconut got
the convicts also to lay out the estate in coconut
plants. He was now 55 and lived on the estate at
Irois with his wife, Anna, and the unmarried children and they were to remain there until her death
in 1876. He used to ride on horseback two or three
times a week to La Brea, to look after his asphalt
business, for he stuck to it through thick and thin,
and indeed it was asphalt which eventually made
him a wealthy man. After six years the Government decided to close down the Convict station
and put the estate up for auction. Stollmeyer was
the only bidder, but as a matter of principle bid
$7,000 for it, which he knew was what the Gov-
ernment had paid for it in the first place. Besides
the production of coconuts, Stollmeyer set up a
brick yard at Irois estate from which he sent thousands of bricks by lighter to Port of Spain to build
a whole range of houses at Picadilly to the east of
the city.

Conrad Frederick had twelve children, the
first three born in the United States, two in England and the remainder in Trinidad. Five of them
died in childhood. Their mother, at least on some
occasions, had an easy delivery. In bringing up
the children she was assisted by a coloured nurse
(or as Conrad called her 'a governess'). Anna was
an extremely kind and caring mother, but had
quite a hard time since her husband was often so

busy with his various enterprises. She would say to her eldest son Charles: "You must look after your brothers and sisters, because your father is wrapped up in his work" - and Charles tried to fulfill her request faithfully. In 1858 Anna's widowed sister and two children spent several months with the Stollmeyer's, but this was Anna's only contact with her family as her husband was to leave Trinidad only 33 years after he first came to the island - "one of the finest spots on the globe. The resources are immense, the climate beautiful".

Conrad treasured his family: "As to Paradise, if it is not within us and within the circle of our little families and a few proven friends, it has little chance to come from the outer world"; but he also loved his work: "I believe I have inherited the love and the gift of making money". And things could sometimes be a little more difficult than usual. For instance, at Irois he insisted on a vegetarian diet - even cow's milk had to be replaced by coconut milk. For years, the day before the fortnightly mailboat left for England, he became agitated and virtually locked himself away, for he had "the bad habit never to write in advance so that the mailing days became a kind of beastly threat". Like most of the German wives in Trinidad, (with a few notable exceptions) Anna could, however, count on her husband being faithful to her, for on the whole the Germans did not acquire (in the fashion of some French creoles) what has been called "an estate morality" which required a "spare wheel".

Conrad Frederick was a man about five foot five inches in height, broad and deep-chested and very strong for his size. He was ambidextrous, a total abstainer and a non-smoker. Even up to the end of his life he spoke English with a German accent, though he was fluent at patois. His health was good during almost the whole of his long career. He was sixty-three when his wife died in 1876. After her death, he returned to Port of Spain and undertook the first of a number of trips to Europe and the United States. While in England in 1878 he met and married a very engaging lady named Routledge. Unfortunately she died in New York on the journey back to Trinidad. Conrad remained a widower until 1886 when he wed Elizabeth Tench, a lady from Dominica considerably younger than himself, and who out-lived him.

From the 1860's Stollmeyer had entered into partnership with Finlayson in a company to export asphalt. Both partners did extremely well as asphalt became more and more popular in Europe and the States for the making of roads. On his trips abroad Stollmeyer used the opportunity to consolidate business arrangements and make new deals. While Finlayson leased part of the Lake, fortunately for the firm much of the production came from Stollmeyer's lands some distance from the Lake. And so in 1887 when Previte and Barber by rather devious methods obtained from the Trinidad Government a monopoly on mining pitch from the Lake, including a clause forbidding the mining of pitch within three miles of the Lake, they would still have been faced with competition from Stollmeyer. Consequently they made an agreement with Stollmeyer that on condition that he did not work or ship asphalt from his own lands he would be given 10 cents a ton on all shipments. He thus acquired a substantial revenue each year until his death.

In 1851 there was founded at Utica New York, the Order of Good Templars, a society of abstainers whose members took a pledge against the consumption of alcohol. It 1868 this was introduced into Great Britain. In Trinidad, for many years Stollmeyer had been a one-man anti-alcoholic movement, in spite of the derision and laughter of some of his associates. He now joined with two Englishmen who were living in Trinidad, and contacted the Order in England to inform them of a group he had set up in Trinidad. William Tomkins, Special Deputy of the Grand Lodge of England, came out to Trinidad in 1874 and commissioned Stollmeyer as the First District Deputy of the island. With the German's enthusiastic backing and by enlisting a few of his business friends, he was successful in establishing a number of branches, including one among the military at the St James Barracks. In the 1880's a Good Templar Hall was built in Port of Spain.

Conrad wrote his mother regularly until her death and kept some contact with the rest of the family in Ulm. The magnificent Gothic Cathedral there had been begun in 1377, and in 1844 the work of completion and restoration (of the then Lutheran-owned building) was undertaken and was to be completed in 1890. As a loyal if not

exactly enthusiastic son of the city, Stollmeyer
(and his son Charles) at great cost donated a
stained-glass window to the Cathedral. This de-
picted the adoration of the Infant Jesus and as
was the custom of the time the members of the
Stollmeyer family represent the Biblical characters. A watercolor of this window is in the possession of the family. The inscription at the bottom
of the window is in German and reads:

Donated Anno Domini 1891
by Conrad.F.Stollmeyer
born in Ulm
and His Son Carl F. Stollmeyer
from Trinidad B.W.I.

Conrad, who had always been a Theist and
not really a Lutheran, was very taken up with the
new Philosophy or Religion, founded in 1875 in
New York City by Helena Petrovna Blavtsky, and
known as Theosophy. A mixture of philosophy,
pseudo-science, eastern mysticism and esoteric
speculation, it appealed very much to the old man,
who acquired a number of volumes on the subject
called "The Ancient Wisdom" (1899). His son
Charles also became very interested in Theosophy believing it had the answer to life's problems,
and added many more books to the library.
Conrad claimed to have studied all religions but
he practised none. However, he contributed to the
construction of many churches in Trinidad, belonging to all sorts of cults - for instance, donating wood
to construct the Roman Catholic presbytery at La

Brea.

Stollmeyer was now a very rich man and he increased his wealth by further investments in companies that appealed to his scientific mind. He was a director of Trinidad's first Telephone Company and was also a large shareholder in the Electric Company. The Cocorite tramline with its mule-drawn trams, (though it was his original plan to have it run by electricity) owed its laying down to his energy and perseverance in the face of powerful opposition. He erected modern works for the production of Coconut oil for cooking, at La Basse just outside of Port of Spain - "the oil is genuine, of good quality and entirely free from adulteration. It possesses a pale colour and an agreeable natural flavor".

In the 1880's, Stollmeyer was one of the Vice-Presidents of the Universal Peace Union of Philadelphia, the aim of which was to persuade the rulers of the various countries to live at peace. When he was over 75 years of age, in 1889, he travelled to Caracas to see the chief ministers in the Venezuelan Government, in an effort to improve relations between Great Britain and the South American country, which had been soured by the Venezuela-British Guiana boundary dispute.

A great many people take it for granted that a man over age 40 has already established an identity and is rooted in a rut, but Stollmeyer even when twice that age was ready to undertake the unexpected. Along with his old friend Rapsey he launched into a scheme for the large scale planting of bamboo at Aranguez for the production of paper.

Conrad was appointed an acting member of the Legislative Council of Trinidad on the 19th November 1894, to replace W.S.Robertson who was out of the island. He was present in December for the vote on the motion for elected members to the Legislative Council proposed by the aged Louis de Verteuil, and he voted in favor - the motion being lost by 12 votes to 6. He was never confirmed as a member of the Legislature (being retired on the return of Robertson in April 1895) and claimed that this was due to his protest against the Military estimates - a small sum of money being voted every year for the Volunteers. No doubt due to his anti-war principles, Stollmeyer had proposed that the money for the Volunteers be struck from the estimates for 1895, but failed to find a seconder. Thereupon at the next meeting, he presented a protest to be sent to the Secretary of State for the colonies, giving 8 reasons why the money should not have been voted. One of them reads truthfully but unacceptably:

> Because the Volunteer Corps are like Cricket, Polo and other sports a matter of amusement for our young men, and as such ought to be supported by voluntary contributions, and not by taxation of the mass of the people, who have no need for them.

At the Council meeting of 25th February 1895, he proposed a motion, seconded by Dr de Verteuil, 'that the Electric Light and Power Company be required to lay the Electric wires underground and not overhead on poles'. Unfortunately, only Bell-Smythe supported the motion which was lost 12 to 3, and so today our towns are a monstrous mess of overhead wires.

On a trip to Europe with his third wife Elizabeth Tench, while staying in a hotel Conrad had a terrible fall. His sight was not good and he stepped into a lift-shaft not noticing that the lift had gone down. He fell down on top of the lift and broke his leg and other bones and was laid up for some time. When he was well enough to travel back to Trinidad, they made friends with a Miss Sybil Gray who was travelling on the same boat. She was to become Conrad's secretary for many years, writing all his letters and reading to him. She could do this easily, as he was then living at 112 Picton Street and her parents' house was just across the road from his. Unfortunately, one day when Conrad was visiting his son at Santa Cruz, No. 112 Picton Street was burnt to the ground. Everything was lost in this fire, including very lovely possessions, silver and ornaments as well as all his private papers. In spite of his philosophical beliefs, when he saw the ruins of his home, poor Conrad wept bitterly. After the fire, the family moved to a house at the top of Picton street and he lived there for the remainder of his life.

When he was nearly 90 years of age, he had an operation for cataract which was successful. In 1903 he got the Asphalt Company to carry him to Brighton (La Brea) in their launch. On arrival at Brighton he was carried up to the Pitch Lake in a chair. On the Lake he stood up and declared: "Godfather, I want to thank you for all you have done for me". Up to the commencement of his last illness he was most active in keeping an eye on the progress of his many business concerns. His health, however, began to deteriorate, and having appointed his son, Dr. Arthur Stollmeyer as his sole attorney, he left for Barbados on the 5th February 1904, for a complete rest, but he only became worse and was advised to return. It soon became obvious that the end was only a question of a short time. Out of consideration for him, Picton Street near his home was covered with sawdust, so that he would not be bothered by the sound of the passing horses and carriages. On Saturday 30th April 1904, a few days before his ninety-first birthday, he passed away quietly in the early morning, conscious almost to the last, leaving a wife and three children (out of twelve) to mourn his loss. The funeral took place on Saturday afternoon at All Saints Church. At the close of the church service at the graveside, the customary Masonic rites and honors were performed, the funeral being conducted by the Lodge of the United Brothers of which the deceased was for very many years a member. All the other sister lodges were represented.

At his death, *Creole Bitters* paid the following tribute to him, every word of which rings true:

> Mr Stollmeyer was a man who was born to succeed in life but who was also bound to have to overcome opposition and difficulties before achieving success. He was born to succeed on account of his clear and sound judgement, his

industry, energy, indomitable perseverance; he was the more bound to meet the vicissitudes which are the ordinary lot on earth of all men of strong mind and will, who are the uncompromising enemies of tyranny and injustice and the lover of Temperance and Peace.

Although not cut off from the German community in Trinidad, Stollmeyer was never closely identified with them. He was most at home with the English creoles, since he had during his career worked at many Government jobs. Nevertheless, his opposition as a liberal to the ultra-conservative Charles William Warner (until his death in 1887) was well known. Sad to say, the French creoles hardly associated with him. Few attended his funeral and he was sometimes the butt of their jokes, such as that his coconut oil was useless for cooking and useful only as a mosquito repellent.

But above all, the German was a highly individualistic man who enjoyed his eccentricities. The *Mirror* considered that: "He was a remarkable man and his life teaches two great lessons, first, what perseverance and hard work can do and second, that all honest work is honourable". Conrad Stollmeyer lived 90 years, eleven months and twenty days. Up to late in his life he was a man of demonic energy and inexhaustible resourcefulness. His time extended from seventeen years before the first train to one year after the first aeroplane; from when "kissing was not to be taken lightly" to the Edwardian times of enjoyable embracing; from an undeveloped island of 60,000 people to a Trinidad on the edge of the oil explosion. He died owing no man.

Of his progeny, six died as children. The eldest boy, named after his father Conrad Frederick, studied to be a Baptist preacher. He was being trained by a Rev.Law and it was while taking services and preaching to the people of La Brea, that he contracted malaria and died, at the age of 22.   Sophia, his sister, married Louis Geofroy and they lived in Port of Spain. During the years that her father dwelt at Irois, the two youngest boys, James Arthur Rex and Andre Blasini, during the school term lived with their married sister and attended Queen's Royal College. In holiday time they went up and down by the steamer, for the estate was not a very enticing place for teen-age boys.

Arthur (as he was called) won the island scholarship from Q.R.C. in 1875, and studied medicine in Scotland. He did brilliantly in his early examinations but proceeded to fail his finals ten years running. Finally his father refused to support him any longer and his brother, Charles Fourier, offered him just one more chance. The family tradition has it that Arthur had become an alcoholic but it seems probable that like many wealthy aristocrats in the United Kingdom at this time, he had become a 'professional student', finding University life far more pleasant than qualifying and having to go to work. He passed his finals both at Edinburgh and Glasgow with the highest possible grades, an L.R.C.P. and M.R.C.S. from Edinburgh University and an L.C.P. & S. from Glasgow, and returned to Trinidad to prac-

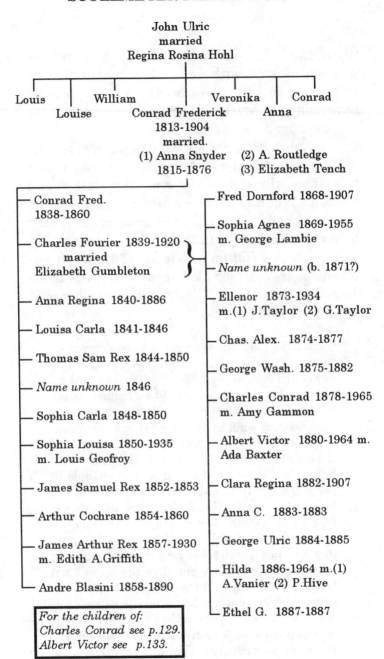

John Ulric
married
Regina Rosina Hohl

Louis
Louise
William
Conrad Frederick
1813-1904
married.
(1) Anna Snyder   (2) A. Routledge
1815-1876   (3) Elizabeth Tench
Veronika
Anna
Conrad

— Conrad Fred.
1838-1860

— Charles Fourier 1839-1920
married
Elizabeth Gumbleton

— Anna Regina 1840-1886

— Louisa Carla 1841-1846

— Thomas Sam Rex 1844-1850

— *Name unknown* 1846

— Sophia Carla 1848-1850

— Sophia Louisa 1850-1935
m. Louis Geofroy

— James Samuel Rex 1852-1853

— Arthur Cochrane 1854-1860

— James Arthur Rex 1857-1930
m. Edith A.Griffith

— Andre Blasini 1858-1890

— Fred Dornford 1868-1907

— Sophia Agnes 1869-1955
m. George Lambie

— *Name unknown* (b. 1871?)

— Ellenor 1873-1934
m.(1) J.Taylor (2) G.Taylor

— Chas. Alex. 1874-1877

— George Wash. 1875-1882

— Charles Conrad 1878-1965
m. Amy Gammon

— Albert Victor 1880-1964 m.
Ada Baxter

— Clara Regina 1882-1907

— Anna C. 1883-1883

— George Ulric 1884-1885

— Hilda 1886-1964 m.(1)
A.Vanier (2) P.Hive

— Ethel G. 1887-1887

For the children of:
Charles Conrad see p.129.
Albert Victor see p.133.

tise in 1892. Though married to Edith Griffith he was not blessed with any children. He died in 1930. His brother, Andre, became a civil engineer, never married, worked in the Government service and died aged 31, of tuberculosis.

Apart from Sophia, the only girl who survived to adulthood was Anna Regina. She was a tall, physically strong and mentally alert young woman. When her mother died in 1876 and the family moved to Port of Spain, she elected to stay behind at Irois and run the coconut estate of 672 acres. A description of her, in 1881, when she was 40 years old, (she died aged 46) is given in his diary by Abbé Massé, the Roman Catholic priest of La Brea and Cedros.

Near Irois lives the terrible Miss Stolmeyer in charge of an estate of coconuts belonging to her father old Stolmeyer. She handles the cutlass like a negro, mounts a horse like a female equestrian performer in a circus and makes her obstinate negroes walk in line like a shepherd makes his sheep walk. She herself holds the reins of the estate. It is she who does all the sales. She has a shop in which she sells all the victuals to her workers. In fact she alone does the work of four or five men. She does not use mounts except on the estate. Her journeys in the vicinity are done on foot; eight or ten hours in the same day does not frighten her and after having done one such long journey she does not appear too tired. She takes nothing however to give her nerves, because at her house no spirits ever enter. Miss Stolmeyer's father is white. Never will he have a black man at his table. His daughter is not so exclusive. She was very agreeable

and full of concern for Mr Louis Gervais (a
coloured man) who merits it. We all lunched with
her.

One day somebody came into the house to insult
her old father. She took the misguided individual
by the seat of his pants and threw him outside.
Another time she had to complain about the
schoolmaster of Erin who had spoken ill of her.
She met him passing on horseback on her estate
without authorization. She caught him by a leg,
threw him to the ground and administered a vol-
ley of kicks and cuffs.

All the Stollmeyers living today in Trinidad
are descended from Charles Fourier Stollmeyer,
Conrad Frederick's second son, born in the United
States on 3rd September 1839.   He came to
Trinidad with his parents via England. During
his boyhood days, the family were poor and strug-
gling. He went to a Wesleyan school until he was
thirteen years of age. He left then to go to work.
The school fees amounted to 5 cents per week. This
sum his mother gave him to hand to the teacher,
but often he did not and on the day for payment
he did not attend. In after years, this pricked his
conscience so much that he went to the Wesleyan
minister, confessed his fault and promised to give
$20 to the funds each year. This he called "con-
science money". He began giving it around the
year 1867 and continued until the year of his death
in 1920.

During his young working days, Charles
Fourier (Fourier is the name of a French philoso-
pher, admired by Charles Conrad Stollmeyer) did

many jobs. Planting tobacco at Cocorite, superintending the laying of the telegraph line between Port of Spain and San Fernando, visiting all the sugar estates between the capital and Oropouche, for the purpose of buying and transporting the old iron to be sold as scrap. Both these jobs he did walking. With the laying of the telegraph line, he returned each evening to his home in town until the line reached as far as Chaguanas. Thereafter, he camped with his men at the end of each day. (These were the days before the railway had been laid down, and the usual means of transport to Chaguanas from Port of Spain was by sea.) With the purchasing of old iron, he often slept at the estate which he would reach by late afternoon. Once he walked from Port of Spain to Oropouche. He left one afternoon; walking through the night, he arrived at San Fernando next morning; he had some breakfast and then continued on to Oropouche. From Oropouche he returned to San Fernando the same day before taking a rest. Then he hired a mule, rode back to Port of Spain, - and had to go to bed for two days!

Charles Fourier had severe malaria in his youth and throughout his life was thin and wiry. He never weighed more than 126 pounds. Full of energy, he never spared himself or his strength. His one (foolish) luxury was heavy smoking. He worked also in conjunction with his father in the making of asphalt tiles. They were laid on some of the pavements of Port of Spain and in the yards of a few people.

During the 1860's when he was in his twenties, he spent much of his time at La Brea helping his father in the asphalt work and acquiring certain lots of land in the village. At this time Thomas A. Finlayson, sugar planter, businessman and later member of the Legislative Council, was having a great deal of trouble with his shipments of asphalt and as an experiment hired Charles to undertake the work. A few days later Charles met Finlayson in his office in Port of Spain. The latter, very surprised, told him: "Stollmeyer what on earth are you doing up here? I thought I contracted you to load the vessel at La Brea?" "Well", said Charles, "not alone is she loaded but look out your window and see her in the harbour waiting for her dispatch papers." Finlayson was so pleased, that a permanent agreement was made for Charles to handle all loading of crude and refined asphalt, which agreement continued in force till 1930, and out of it came a fortune for Finlayson and his successors and for the Stollmeyer family.

Week after week, particularly in the early years, Charles would leave Port of Spain in a four-oared whale-boat at 1 a.m. on Mondays, returning home on Saturday evenings. Later on, he needed to go only once a fortnight, and by then a steamer was plying from the capital to La Brea; and by then too Charles was in charge also of asphalt exploitation and loading for Lord Dundonald.

Charles Stollmeyer was married in 1867. Elizabeth Gumbleton arrived from England with her younger sister Harriet in that year. She had not been here for three months when Stollmeyer met her and after a six weeks engagement, married her. Charles (like his father before him) could be quite difficult at times but Elizabeth was a wonderful wife and a wonderful mother. She was to bear thirteen children, of whom seven survived into adulthood. The couple were happily married for 53 years, and Elizabeth survived her husband for another 13 years, and died aged 86. For the first six years of her marriage she had it fairly hard to make both ends meet. After that year the family lived on 'easy street', at first in London Street, then in Newtown, then in Edward Street and finally in Belmont. The young boys in the family enjoyed Belmont, swimming in a little stream and two of them riding a donkey to school in Port of Spain, but their mother did not like the place, so in 1884 the family built a house at 'Mon Valmont' in Santa Cruz and made their home there. They remained there for ten years and then moved one and a half miles up the valley, to 'La Regalada'.

This change in residence had important repercussions for Charles Fourier's business. Unlike his father, Conrad Frederick, who preferred buying shares, Charles liked to invest in land, and living on one cocoa estate in Santa Cruz Valley he gradually acquired more and more. By 1911, in this beautiful, cool, well-watered valley, graced by the brilliant red of the immortelle shade trees in the dry season, he owned Curucaie, Santa Anna, La Deseada, La Regalada, San Rafael, Mon Valmont estates (a total of 5,000 acres) as well as St Sauveur at Gran Couva and San Carlos at

Guanapo, and Perseverance at Oropouche, besides Irois estate (under coconuts) which he inherited from his father. The surrounding mountains of the Santa Cruz valley not planted in cocoa, had quantities of valuable timber, cedar, cyp, mahogany, olivier. Up to 1900 almost all the people spoke patois and it was difficult to find a labourer who was fluent in English. The road over the Saddle to Maraval was opened only around 1909, so to get to Port of Spain via Maraval one had to go by horseback.

By 1892 Charles was an extremely wealthy man and bought three acres and a large bungalow on the St Ann's Road (now 9 Queen's Park East) as a town house, and the family lived between Santa Cruz and St Ann's Road, keeping up the two establishments till most of the children were grown up, when Charles Fourier and his wife moved permanently to Port of Spain. She loved her beautiful home looking out on the Queen's Park Savannah to the west.

In 1903 William Gordon Gordon, the wealthy Scottish merchant, began the erection of 'Knowsley', the magnificent mansion facing north to the Queen's Park Savannah. And in the same year lots were laid out on the lands of the old St. Clair sugar estate (later, the Government Stock Farm) the area immediately to the west of the Queen's Park Savannah. By September 1904 to the amazement of the populace of Port of Spain, enormous buildings of a type never before erected in Trinidad were seen to be going up on these lots. Apart from Queen's Royal College and the resi-

dence of the Roman Catholic Archbishop (reflect-
ing the triumphalism of the late nineteenth century and necessarily imitated by the Anglican
Bishop), four other residences were in the course
of construction. The conservative French creole
planters who for more than a century had spent
their money on gracious living and lavish entertaining and erected only wooden houses, called the
new area 'Stoneybroke Avenue', for they suspected
that the cost of construction would leave the owners bankrupt. A young English official more
bluntly described the row of buildings as 'Lunacy
Lane'.

These magnificent creations were erected
to endure, to be lived in, but above all to be spec-
tacular - to be seen. They were to be the residences of the new Trinidad society, of people who
were once only on the borders of French creole society - mansions built for a Scottish merchant, an
English Bishop, an Irish Archbishop, a Venezuelan Spaniard, a Corsican businessman, a coloured
French creole and a German entrepreneur. These
mansions did as much to mark the change in social structure as the decline of cocoa, the First
World War and the death of the French language
in Trinidad. The only one to compete with the new
society was the old Chatelaine of Champs Elysées,
Madame de Boissiere, whose family ironically,
because they had been Huguenots and money
lenders, were themselves once on the fringe. The
German involved in this mansion-mania was of
course, Charles Fourier Stollmeyer.

What precisely made Charles undertake

the building of the edifice now called Killarney or Stollmeyer' Castle, is difficult to know. It was designed after a part of Balmoral Castle by the Scottish architect Robert Gillies of the firm Taylor and Gillies, Taylor being Charles' son-in-law. It was completed by 1904. It is of imported brick trimmed with local limestone and the marble for the gallery which surrounds the ground floor was imported from Italy. The ceilings on the ground-floor are of plaster of Paris, the gesso work of an Italian craftsman, and add to the charm of the well-proportioned rooms. The floors and harp-shaped staircase are of purpleheart imported from Guyana. The light, filtering through the stained glass windows to the east gives an etherial effect to the whole home. A spiral staircase leads to the tower from which a panoramic view may be had of Port of Spain. In the early years of the century the Stollmeyers could look out to the south east to see the Polo matches played every Tuesday and Friday afternoons in the Savannah opposite Whitehall, the spectacle being enhanced every first Friday, when the Police Band attended. If Charles had intended this house as a gift for his wife, it was an expensive mistake . She found it far too elaborate for her simple tastes and her husband was to give it to their son Conrad when he got married.

Like his father before him, Charles was a Theosophist and a teetotaller, but from early manhood to his sixty-third year he was an extremely heavy smoker of cigars. This excessive smoking affected his nerves and digestion, so he went to

England for treatment. He was advised to smoke less but he gave it up altogether. Both his complaints lessened considerably and he lived on till 1920 when he was a few days short of his eighty-first birthday. He was a scrupulously fair man and generous to those whom he considered deserving of it, and as hard a worker as his father had been, a characteristic which he passed on to some of his children. His son Charles Conrad relates the following story:

> One day when Finlayson was sitting in a chair at the door of his office, looking out on the sea, my father strolled up with me at his side. Finlayson took me on his knee. I was only nine years of age, and he asked, "Charlie, what do you intend to do with this boy?" To which my father replied, "That boy will grow up to be the working jackass of the family, the same as I have been." Well, he had been, and I have been and still am.

In his old age, Charles Fourier had a terrible mania for routine. He would clap his hands and call until whomever he wanted came and he would get very impatient if they did not come right away. Every morning he would have a drive to Diego Martin in his carriage and as he passed Killarney, his grandchildren would look out to get a glimpse of him. He would sit looking out of the window of his house every afternoon and at 6 o'clock start fidgeting for his wife to come home. He would say she was an angel if she was punctual and call her the worst names if she were at all late. In 1920 he fell and broke his leg and was never the same again, dying that same year. All the family were very sad when he died. His children loved and admired him greatly and were always very proud to speak of their father.

Of Charles Fourier's four daughters, three married (all surviving him) but the fourth died at age twenty-five. Three sons survived to adulthood. The eldest of these Frederick Dornford, was the black sheep of the family, for after completing his studies at Queen's Royal College, he refused to work with his father. His brother Charles Conrad later wrote of him.

My eldest brother Fred, ten years my senior, never liked work, and that was a great worry to his parents. He just liked being alone on the estates, never doing any work. Finally he went to live on the Guamal estate with Eric Bonval, the overseer. He grew vegetables occasionally in an effort to occupy his time. He was the biggest of us all, five foot eleven inches tall and broad in proportion. He was strong, being able to carry from the mountain garden to the estate house, a full bag of tannias, and being out in the open, gave him a burnt brown complexion. So much so that once when my father went up to the estate to see him, he my father, saw a man coming into the yard with a heavy bag over his shoulder, he shouted, "Hey, man. where is Mr Fred?" The man, who was Fred, answered, "I am here Papa". He was very good-natured, generous and kind to those around him. His great ambition was to learn to play the clarinet, so for this purpose he often rode a pony into town, a distance of eight miles, to have lessons. We other children liked him. He told us more than once that he was a bad example to us and that any other father would have turned him out. Whenever he was ill, he would come to stay with us, either at La Regalada or at 9 Queen's Park East, so that our uncle, Dr. Arthur Stollmeyer could treat him. He died in 1907, aged thirty-nine.

Charles Conrad and his younger brother, Albert Victor, both went to school in Port of Spain, to Miss Briggs in Charles Street, and then to college in England for six years. At age sixteen, Charles returned to Trinidad to help his father in business, and after a course in agricultural chemistry at the Government Laboratory, went to work on the cocoa estates. Albert who arrived back two years later also worked at the cocoa properties.

The *Humming Bird* of 25th June 1904 published the following:

A telegram on Wednesday announced the wedding of Mr. Charles Conrad Stollmeyer to Amy, daughter of the Rev. R.E. and Mrs. Gammon, late of St John's Church, Pembroke Street. The honeymoon is being passed on the continent. On Wednesday, a flag was floating from the tower of Killarney, Mr Stollmeyer's new house on the Savannah, in honour of the happy event.

Two years later, Albert was married to Ada Baxter. Their father gave each son two or three cocoa estates, Killarney was to be Charles' residence and Mon Valmont in Santa Cruz, Albert's. In addition, Charles received $40,000 and Albert $80,000 (a very large sum in those days) so they both had a good start in their married lives. In

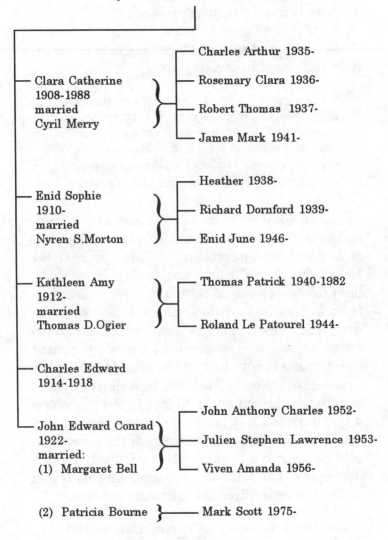

Charles Conrad 1879-1965
married
Amy Kathleen Gammon 1881-1969

Clara Catherine
1908-1988
married
Cyril Merry

Charles Arthur 1935-

Rosemary Clara 1936-

Robert Thomas 1937-

James Mark 1941-

Enid Sophie
1910-
married
Nyren S.Morton

Heather 1938-

Richard Dornford 1939-

Enid June 1946-

Kathleen Amy
1912-
married
Thomas D.Ogier

Thomas Patrick 1940-1982

Roland Le Patourel 1944-

Charles Edward
1914-1918

John Edward Conrad
1922-
married:
(1) Margaret Bell

John Anthony Charles 1952-

Julien Stephen Lawrence 1953-

Viven Amanda 1956-

(2) Patricia Bourne — Mark Scott 1975-

the Stollmeyer tradition they were both very hard workers throughout their careers.

Charles Conrad, who was popularly known as 'C.C.', shared in the religious beliefs of his father and grandfather. He wrote:

> While I profess to be a Christian inasmuch as I try to follow, as much as my present development allows, the teaching and philosophy of Jesus, the most perfect man who has been born on this earth, yet I am a Theosophist, believing ardently in retribution, reincarnation and progress.

In addition to cocoa, C.C. had also a stake in asphalt, inherited from his father and grandfather and an interest in oil. Though he later leased out the oil rights on his land or sold the land to the various oil companies, he at first had tried to undertake drilling himself. The well was drilled at Perseverance estate, Guapo, and due to a fire, drilling was suspended till new equipment could be obtained. But on the 5th May 1912 the pressure of the oil below blew the well, and oil and sand were thrown up to 80 feet in the air, about 4,000 barrels a day gushing out and flowing into the Vance River which, because of the exceptionally heavy rains, could not be controlled. Beeby-Thompson, the famous oil pioneer and no friend of Stollmeyer's, gives the following account.

> Stollmeyer, owner of Perseverance Estate, Guapo, known to have promising oil potentialities, determined to drill himself, when others had struck oil in the vicinity. He had provided himself with a second-hand antiquated rig and en-

trusted its working to some unqualified but cheap operators, who ferreted a well down somehow with quaint ante-diluvian tools. At a depth of only 250 feet, a rich oil sand was unexpectedly struck and such a violent and sustained outburst of heavy oil followed that the immediate vicinity became flooded with oil which ran into the nearby Vance River and out into the Gulf, polluting everything along the river course and turning the clean sandy beach into an awful mess. The offer of Beeby-Thompson to shut down the well was declined. Stollmeyer said that "he did not intend to interfere with the actions of nature"; consequently most of the oil was lost.

C.C. had over sixty years of extremely happy married life. For the first four years there were no children and his wife occupied herself with creating a beautiful garden; in 1904 at the annual Agricultural show she received honorable mention for her cut roses in baskets. Then in 1908 the children began coming, and the family was blessed with three girls and two boys. As the family grew up, C.C. used La Regalada in Santa Cruz as a country house. His daughters got married (see family tree) and the wedding receptions were held at Killarney. An interesting story, the truth of which cannot be vouched for but which shows the mentality of Trinidad society, tells how at the wedding celebration only juices and non-alcoholic drinks were served but that the next morning (for some mysterious reason) the gardener found the fountain full of empty rum and whisky bottles! C.C.'s son John qualified in medicine at McGill University, Montreal, and has been practising in

Trinidad for many years. Charles Conrad died in 1965 aged 87 years, his funeral service being held in the hall at Killarney.

Albert Victor, the younger brother of C.C., lived at Mon Valmont estate at Santa Cruz and at first was mainly a cocoa planter. He knew the trees that grew in the fields around his home 'personally', and could be seen most afternoons trimming them with his cutlass. In the late twenties he was involved in the merchandising of cocoa, and when the market crashed in New York he lost all his assets and was forced to mortgage his home and property - a virtual bankrupt. Being a typical Stollmeyer he did not take matters lying down. Helped by Barclay's Bank he made a new start in citrus. He could not send the last four members of his family abroad to university, and when bush fires used to threaten his new enterprise he would scamper up the hillside (all 120 pounds of him) with his family to put out the fires. The children would spend many hours wrapping and packing by hand 'Humming Bird' brand grapefruit, for export to Bermuda and Canada. In 1929, Albert, who was undoubtedly the major pioneer of the citrus industry in Trinidad, formed the Cooperative Citrus Growers Association of which he became the first Secretary-Manager. The Association moved from strength to strength. By 1965 it handled 1.3 million crates of grapefruit and oranges. Stollmeyer was elected to Trinidad's first elected Legislature in 1925.

Ada, his wife, was a woman of rare beauty and poise and presided over the home like the Vic-

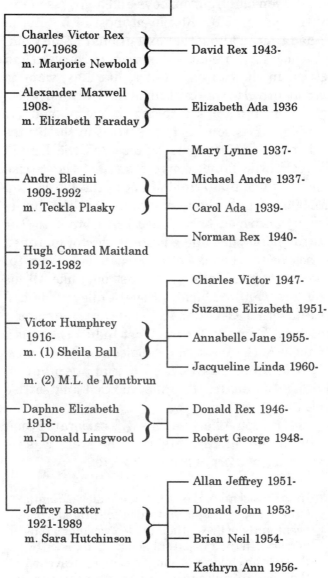

Albert Victor 1880-1964
married
Ada Kate Baxter 1879-1974

Charles Victor Rex
1907-1968
m. Marjorie Newbold
— David Rex 1943-

Alexander Maxwell
1908-
m. Elizabeth Faraday
— Elizabeth Ada 1936

Andre Blasini
1909-1992
m. Teckla Plasky
— Mary Lynne 1937-
— Michael Andre 1937-
— Carol Ada 1939-
— Norman Rex 1940-

Hugh Conrad Maitland
1912-1982

Victor Humphrey
1916-
m. (1) Sheila Ball
— Charles Victor 1947-
— Suzanne Elizabeth 1951-
— Annabelle Jane 1955-
— Jacqueline Linda 1960-

m. (2) M.L. de Montbrun

Daphne Elizabeth
1918-
m. Donald Lingwood
— Donald Rex 1946-
— Robert George 1948-

Jeffrey Baxter
1921-1989
m. Sara Hutchinson
— Allan Jeffrey 1951-
— Donald John 1953-
— Brian Neil 1954-
— Kathryn Ann 1956-

torian matriarch that she was. She bore her husband seven children, six boys and a girl (see family tree page 133). Rex lived most of his life in Canada, as an altogether exceptional Trade Commissioner for Trinidad. Alex, went to Harvard and settled in the States. Andre, like Rex, went to Dartmouth. He was captain of the University soccer team and on his return home played for Trinidad. His son Michael settled in the States and it was his son who represented the United States in the famous match against the 'Strike Squad' which put Trinidad out of the World Cup in 1990. Hugh, the fourth brother in the family was a confirmed bachelor, a contributor to *The Beacon* magazine, and a painter. Victor qualified as a solicitor, but is better known as a West Indian cricketer. Jeffrey, the last boy, like all his brothers went to Queen's Royal College. He had an altogether exceptional cricket career as opener, and later Captain, for the West Indies. He was a member of the West Indies Selection Committee, a prominent businessman and member of Trinidad's Senate. Daphne married and settled in Canada.

In 1956 Albert and his wife celebrated their golden wedding anniversary. The event was recorded in the Port of Spain Gazette:

In the peaceful and picturesque Valley of Santa Cruz, a happy couple yesterday celebrated a big event in their lives - their golden wedding anniversary. In their beautiful home, surrounded by their seven children, some of whom had travelled thousands of miles to be with them on this occa-

Charles Conrad Stollmeyer.
The perfect gentleman.

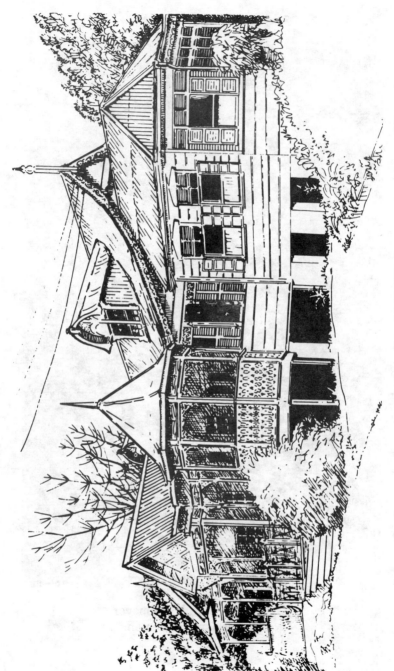

A sketch by Gerald G. Watterson.
"Mon Valmont" in Lower Santa Cruz Valley.

"La Regalada" in Upper Santa Cruz Valley.
Above: A picture taken in the 1890's.
Below: With first floor added in 1909, on birth of Andre.

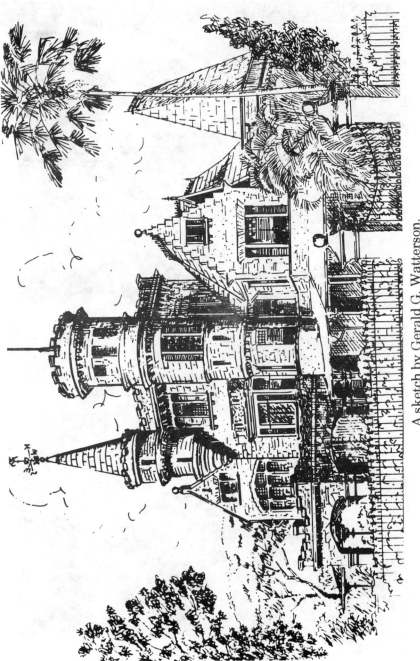

A sketch by Gerald G. Watterson.
"Killarney", Stollmeyer's Castle, built in 1904.

Detail of stained-glass window in Ulm Cathedral,
presented by Conrad and Charles Fourier Stollmeyer in 1890.
According to custom the shepherds have Stollmeyer faces!

"Buen Retiro", the Stollmeyer Home at 9 Queen's Park East.
Charles Fourier's widow, Elizabeth, with her children & grandchildren.

Albert Victor Stollmeyer at work.
Above: At La Regalada estate on "Major". Albert sometimes used a little donkey called *Squilibuey,* patois for a little bird.
Below: In the office in town with his staff. Below the office, was the cocoa store; above, a lookout for ships arriving.

Albert Victor's Golden Wedding Anniversary, 1956.
Back Row: Rex, Alex, Andre, Hugh, Victor, Daphne, Jeffrey.

sion, and with many of their young grandchildren running around, Mr. and Mrs. A.V.Stollmeyer recalled the romantic meeting of fifty years ago which brought them together.

Albert died eight years later, aged 84. The death of his wife in 1974 at the age of 94 marked the end of an era. She lived in the 'Great House' at Mon Valmont until the end. The house, constructed at first as a bungalow in 1880, had a first floor added when the family increased in size. Eventually, the only reason it did not collapse was that the termites in it were standing shoulder to shoulder!

The Stollmeyer family are not the doyen of the German-descended families in Trinidad, but they are certainly the best known, the most prolific and the family that has contributed the most, in a multitude of ways, to their homeland of Trinidad.

Chapter 4

The House of Siegert

These things are to be looked to in a building: that it stands on the right spot; that it be securely founded; that it be successfully executed.
Johann Wolfgang Von Goethe.

Dr. Johann Gottlieb Benjamin Siegert was born in 1796 at Grosswalditz near Loewenberg, in the province of Silesia. He was a brilliant boy and was educated at the Gymnasium of Liegnitz, then studied medicine at the University of Berlin, the capital of Prussia. In 1815 the Emperor Napoleon made his dramatic escape from the little island of Elba, landed on the French coast and once more defied the might of Europe. Then only nineteen years of age, Siegert served as an army surgeon attached to the 3rd Corps de Chasseurs of Magdeburg of the second Regiment of the Prussian infantry, in the campaign of the allies against Napoleon which finally culminated in the Emperor's defeat at Waterloo. For his services he was awarded a campaign medal.

Five years later, in 1820, attracted to the war for freedom from Spanish rule in Venezuela, the doctor with several Prussian young men of noble birth took ship across the Atlantic. Their enrolment in the army was gladly accepted by the Liberator, Bolivar. Eventually, Siegert was as-

signed to the town of Angostura on the Orinoco,
then the capital of the province of Guyana and was
appointed Surgeon General of the military hospital in Guyana. After the war, when Venezuela
had won its freedom from Spain, Siegert settled
in Angostura and practised there as a physician
and surgeon until 1859 when he resigned his practice.

In 1838 Dr.Siegert had been elected a non-
resident member of the Medical society of
Halberstadt to which he had addressed many scientific essays, particularly on the subject of the
medicinal value of tropical herbs and plants, of
which he had made a special study. Indeed, in
1824 (after some years of experimentation) he had
made for his own uses, medicinal and gustatory, a
preparation which he called *Amargo Aromatico*
(Aromatic Bitters). At first he administered it only
to his patients and close friends. But the young
surgeon's bitters soon acquired a reputation not
solely for its medicinal virtues but particularly
because of the special flavor it imparted to cordials, punches and other alcoholic drinks, which
were popular among the hardy seamen and soldiers of the time. It was carried to many parts of
the world (including Trinidad) by the crews of the
sailing ships which called at Angostura and soon
became so popular that Siegert was encouraged
to devote himself to a greater extent to the preparation of this compound.

The bitters was exported for the first time
in 1830 when shipments were sent down the
Orinoco to the German merchants in Trinidad and

then to England, and from that date the actual manufacture of the article may be said to have begun. The bitters became widely known under the name of Angostura Bitters, from the place of its origin - though it is necessary to note that the name of the town was officially changed in 1846 by Act of the Venezuelan Congress, to Ciudad Bolivar (City of Bolivar) in honour of the Liberator.

Angostura, 'the Narrows', is situated up the Orinoco, some 240 miles from the sea, where the mighty river narrows down to a mile wide, and was (in 1870) sixty hours by steamer from Port of Spain, Trinidad, through which all its external trade necessarily flowed; the Trinidad port acting as a trans-shipment center, since large ships could not sail up the Orinoco. In the second half of the nineteenth century, the flat-bottomed steamers and even sailing ships (some engine assisted) transported rubber, tonca beans, alligator skins, feathers from the white egrets found in the swamps for the splendid hats of the society ladies, and hundreds of cattle which had walked for two or three days from all over the Llanos to the river port. At this period, all the principal commercial houses in Angostura (Ciudad Bolivar) were owned by Corsicans or Germans, many of them with family links with Trinidad; so that Siegert had a congenial society to partly occupy him.

Nevertheless, (around 1830), the population of the town was only 9,000 people, so that the doctor had plenty of leisure time available to spend with his common-law-wife, Maria del Pilar Araujo (whom he married on her death-bed). By her he had a number of children, only four of whom survived to adulthood. These were educated in Germany. The three daughters, Carlota, Carmelita and Carolina (See family tree page 141) got married and remained in Europe. The son became a doctor like his father, married Señorita Telesfora Contasti, who bore him six children, and apparently they settled in Caracas.

On the death of his wife Maria, Dr.Siegert married Isabel Doazan, a daughter of Don Carlos Gomez de Zaa. This family were close friends of the famous naturalist Alexander von Humbolt, with whom Dr.Siegert also became very friendly. By his second marriage Dr.Siegert had nine children (see family tree) of whom only six survived. Three of these six were boys, whose names were Carlos Damaso, Alfredo Cornelio and Luis Benjamin del Carmen. All three sons were sent to Germany for their secondary and tertiary education. On their return to Venezuela, they took part in the expansion of the Angostura business to which Dr. Siegert was now devoting himself full time.

By 1850 Dr.Siegert had been presumably eligible for pension and had resigned as surgeon-general of the military hospital in Angostura to give more time to private practice and to his company, which he named J.G.B.Siegert y Hijo (the 'Hijo' - son - being Carlos) and which he felt could develop into a thriving business. With help from his three sons, Carlos Damaso, Alfredo Cornelio and (much later) Luis Benjamin, he expanded his operations by securing external markets. However, as late as 1853 the sale of Bitters did not exceed 20 dozen cases per annum. At the head of advertising and marketing was Carlos Damaso, who was known as the 'Great Advertiser' and he it was who really made the Bitters into a success story. Between 1862 and 1897 he exhibited Angostura Bitters in 18 countries and secured highest honours for the product, for example in the international exhibitions at London (1862), Paris (1867), Vienna (1873), Santiago de Chile (1875), Philadelphia (1876), Sydney (1879) etc. etc. After the Vienna exhibition, when imitations began to hit the market, Siegert's Bitters was identified then (as it still is today) by a facsimile of the signature of Dr J.G.B. Siegert between the two representations of the Medal of Merit (the highest distinction obtainable) awarded in 1873.

When Dr.Siegert died in 1870 in Ciudad Bolivar, Carlos Damaso became the sole owner of the company and the only one in possession of the formula. In 1872 he took into partnership his younger brother Alfredo and changed the name of the firm to Dr.J.G.B. Siegert & Hijos. However, Angostura was an unsuitable centre, from the point of view of exports, since large steamers could not call there, for in the dry season the river dropped fifty feet and steamers were liable to run aground on sand banks. And then there was the constant political unrest in Venezuela during the 1860's - revolts in 1861, 1863, and 1868. On his journeys to advertise the bitters Carlos had become very friendly with Charles William Warner,

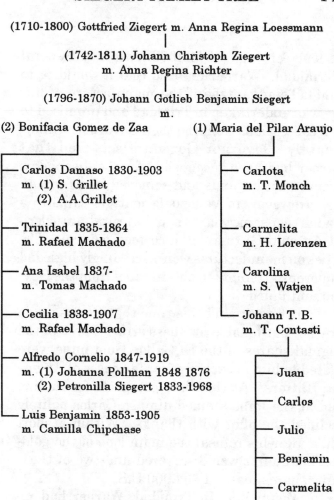

(1710-1800) Gottfried Ziegert m. Anna Regina Loessmann

(1742-1811) Johann Christoph Ziegert
m. Anna Regina Richter

(1796-1870) Johann Gotlieb Benjamin Siegert
m.

(2) Bonifacia Gomez de Zaa   (1) Maria del Pilar Araujo

— Carlos Damaso 1830-1903   — Carlota
  m. (1) S. Grillet   m. T. Monch
     (2) A.A.Grillet

— Trinidad 1835-1864   — Carmelita
  m. Rafael Machado   m. H. Lorenzen

— Ana Isabel 1837-   — Carolina
  m. Tomas Machado   m. S. Watjen

— Cecilia 1838-1907   — Johann T. B.
  m. Rafael Machado   m. T. Contasti

— Alfredo Cornelio 1847-1919
  m. (1) Johanna Pollman 1848 1876   — Juan
     (2) Petronilla Siegert 1833-1968
                         — Carlos

— Luis Benjamin 1853-1905   — Julio
  m. Camilla Chipchase
                         — Benjamin

                         — Carmelita

                         — Carlota

For descendants of:
Carlos Damaso   See page 147.
Alfredo Cornelio See page 147.

the long-serving (1844-1870) Attorney General of Trinidad. Warner realized that it would be to Trinidad's advantage if the manufacture of bitters was undertaken in Trinidad and promised to seek concessions from the then Governor. Unfortunately, Governor Gordon discovered that Warner had been responsible for the disappearance of certain funds and removed him from office. However, in Venezuela matters came to a head in that same year, when the brutal, anti-clerical Antonio Guzman Blanco took control. The duties on manufactures were exceedingly high and numerous attempts to obtain relief from the Government failed.

It was around this time that Carlos made a rather pardonable business error. Three of the original shares of the El Callao Gold mine were offered to him in exchange for ten cases of Angostura Bitters. At this time prospects for finding gold at the mine seemed dim, so Carlos politely declined the offer with thanks. Within a short while after his refusal the main lode of the gold-bearing quartz was discovered and two of those same shares realised $64,000 U.S.

Meanwhile, in Trinidad, Warner had returned to influence and persuaded the Governor, Sir Henry Turner Irving, to introduce and have passed in the Legislative Council an ordinance under which it would be possible for bitters to be manufactured in bond. Once this was in place, the Siegerts decided to leave Venezuela. This was not an easy matter because being born in Venezuela they were by law Venezuelans and had the

Government learnt that they intended to move
their business out of the country they would have
been arrested. They managed however to find a
Captain of a British ship who was prepared to take
them out. The Captain hid them on his ship below decks and they never came on deck until the
ship was in British waters. They landed in
Trinidad and re-established their business there,
where their youngest brother Luis Siegert then
joined them.

The Siegert Brothers at first undertook the
manufacture of their Angostura aromatic bitters
in rented premises at the corner of Charlotte Street
and Marine Square (No. 4 Charlotte Street and No.
37 Marine Square) in Port of Spain. In 1880 they
obtained a loan from the firm of Wilsons and
bought the property 6 & 8 George Street, which
had been the Roman Catholic Presbytery for the
Cathedral, and transferred their factory there.

Angostura Bitters was well known from the
1850's in Trinidad as a remedy for diarrhoea and
upset stomach. But it followed a similar course to
the rum punch (rum, syrup and lime) which was
originally prescribed as a cure for fever and flu.
At first people took it when they were sick, then
when they were getting sick and next when they
were well so they wouldn't get sick, and eventually simply because of its exhilarating taste and
effects. A vigorous advertising campaign in the
Trinidad newspapers encouraged the consumption
of bitters for non-medical reasons. Harrimans, the
agents for the West Indies, at first advertised it
as:

SIEGERT'S BOUQUET
An Agreeable Cordial
ANGOSTURA BITTERS

Later, it was to be marketed as 'Siegert's'; but in the 1870's, 1880's and 1890's, other companies were marketing 'genuine bitters', sometimes advertising in the same newspaper as Angostura. Advertising in Guppy's Almanac for 1880, Harrimans stated:

> The Public is cautioned against imitations bearing names such as per SIEGERT'S prescription, according to SIEGERT, from SIEGETT, from SIEGBERT, SIMPSONS etc etc. as also against all counterfeits under the name of ANGOSTURA BITTERS with a more or less faithful copy of the original label. All these imitations merely tend to deceive and misguide the public, chiefly owing to their low rate of cost and to the use of the word Angostura and consists in the majority of cases of a very inferior mixture, very injurious to health and IN EVERY RESPECT DIFFERING FROM THE GENUINE ANGOSTURA BITTERS.

Legal action had to be taken against them; but even as late as 1894 things were not much better, if we are to judge by another advertisement in Collen's Almanac, which warned the purchasers against 'ANGELSTURA BITTERS' and 'ANGUSTORA BITTERS' and to avoid being misled 'because of BOMBASTIC advertisements with ARABIAN NIGHTS' TALES'. 'These counterfeits though vigorously prosecuted at law, and against which numerous judgements have been obtained, do not cease to spring up anew in one or other form, owing to the immense success the genuine article has secured'.

Interestingly enough, in present day Trinidad almost every home has its bottle of Angostura, primarily for use as a flavouring or cordial or appetizer, but in spite of all the improvements in modern medicine it is still very popular for soothing an upset stomach or settling loose bowels.

In the *Trinidad Chronicle* of 13th April 1878, a poem celebrated the beauty of Angostura Bitters.

THE ANGOSTURA BITTERS

Of Angostura Bitters
The charms I make my lay
In land of Venezuela
That nectar saw the day.
The orange blossoms waving
By Orinoco's waters,
With rum and bark commingling
Produce that first of liquors.

Ambrosial essence gives it
To Xeres golden wine;
Columbia's "Cocktail" hails it,
With flavour made divine.
That best of all the sauces
Men "appetite" do name,
And next to natural causes
From Bitters springs the same.

A Bouquet once it furnished
And "Siegert's" was its name,
That Bouquet's fragrance vanished,

As swiftly as it came.
And yet the immortal Bitters
With never ending fame
Maintains o'er rival liquors
Its flavor and its name.

The oldest girl from Doctor Siegert's second marriage, was called Trinidad. She married in Angostura, Rafael Machado and her sister Ana married his brother Tomas, on the same day in the Doctor's house. When Trinidad died, her widower married her sister Cecilia. As far as we know their families remained in Venezuela. Carlos Damaso had married in Angostura, a girl of French extract, Señorita Grillet. Before her untimely death she bore him six children, the eldest being Petronilla, and all of whom were to join him in Trinidad. On the death of his first wife, he married her sister, Ana Apolonia Grillet, and by her had three children, George Rosalino, Anitica and Albert Anastasio. (See family tree page 147). Alfredo Cornelio, the brother of Carlos, had married Johanna Pollman. She had one daughter and died after her arrival in Trinidad. Alfredo then wed his niece, Petronilla. They had two daughters and a son, Alfredo Galo. Luis Benjamin, Dr. Siegert's youngest son, married Camilla Chipchase in 1878, when the family had already emigrated to Trinidad.

In Trinidad, the Firm of Siegert's Bitters prospered exceedingly. In 1876, 15,160 gallons of Bitters were exported; by 1886 over double that amount, 35,355 gallons. Very many medals and certificates of excellence were obtained in numer-

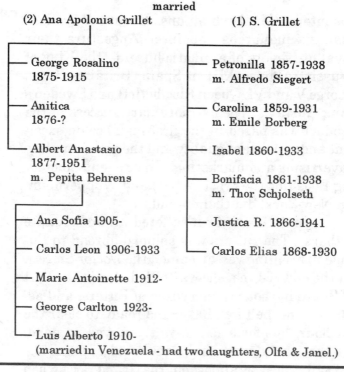

Carlos Damaso 1830-1903
married
(2) Ana Apolonia Grillet   (1) S. Grillet

- George Rosalino 1875-1915
- Anitica 1876-?
- Albert Anastasio 1877-1951 m. Pepita Behrens
  - Ana Sofia 1905-
  - Carlos Leon 1906-1933
  - Marie Antoinette 1912-
  - George Carlton 1923-
  - Luis Alberto 1910- (married in Venezuela - had two daughters, Olfa & Janel.)

- Petronilla 1857-1938 m. Alfredo Siegert
- Carolina 1859-1931 m. Emile Borberg
- Isabel 1860-1933
- Bonifacia 1861-1938 m. Thor Schjolseth
- Justica R. 1866-1941
- Carlos Elias 1868-1930

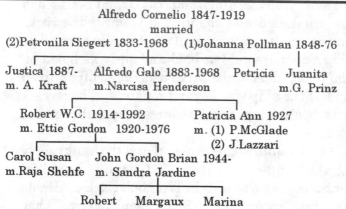

Alfredo Cornelio 1847-1919
married
(2)Petronila Siegert 1833-1968   (1)Johanna Pollman 1848-76

Justica 1887- m. A. Kraft   Alfredo Galo 1883-1968 m.Narcisa Henderson   Petricia   Juanita m.G. Prinz

Robert W.C. 1914-1992 m. Ettie Gordon 1920-1976   Patricia Ann 1927 m. (1) P.McGlade (2) J.Lazzari

Carol Susan m.Raja Shehfe   John Gordon Brian 1944- m. Sandra Jardine

Robert   Margaux   Marina

ous international exhibitions. Eventually no less than six monarchs appointed Angostura their royal purveyors of aromatic bitters - the King of Prussia, Alfonso XIII of Spain, Britain's Kings George V and VI, Queen Elizabeth II and Sweden's King Gustav. The extraordinary success of the product was based in the first instance on excellent and consistent quality and then on first-class advertising and marketing. Their agents, including Boos (for the West Indies) and Wuppermann (in New York) did them proud.

In 1895 the firm suffered an unfortunate setback. The Bitters was shipped abroad to Europe in a sailing vessel named the *Doctor Siegert*. At the end of June, she was fully laden in the Port of Spain harbour with a cargo of Bitters, and asphalt from the Pitch Lake, and ready to clear the harbour, but for a few days there was no wind. On the 4th July a slight breeze sprung up and she set sail. She was almost out the Grand Boca when the wind died and she drifted towards the rocks on the north-western point of Chacachacare. The ship's anchors did not hold and she was holed on the reef. Most of the cargo was taken off or dived up but the ship was beyond repair, and her wreck was broken up and dispersed by subsequent storms.

In spite of this accident and the bankruptcy of their agent in British Guiana, by 1900 Dr.Siegert's three sons in Trinidad, Carlos, Alfredo and Luis were very wealthy men indeed. They were also very charitable to the poor and unfortunate, but their many acts of benevolence, as far as

possible, were never made public. Each one had
their favourite charities: in the case of Luis, it was
the Belmont Reformatory and Industrial school
and the Roman Catholic Church; apart from public charities, Carlos was President and immense
benefactor of the Trinidad Rifle Association and
gave a large number of young men a start in life -
though some of them showed him only ingratitude
or were a disappointment to him; Alfredo was the
one who kept the Belmont Orphanage in solvency
and financed the building of the boys' school (very
recently demolished) to the west of St. Patrick's
R.C. Presbytery, Newtown.

In 1886 Carlos bought *The Hall* which occupied a whole block at Chancery Lane and had
been the residence of Charles William Warner. It
was a charming house with a swimming pool and
a beautiful garden. Carlos set up there the first
tennis court in the island. There were large stables
across the road, (facing east to Chancery Lane),
in which Carlos kept race horses and eleven carriages of various sizes. Carlos brought out a gardener specially from Germany, to look after the
garden.

The main entrance to the building was on
Chancery Lane, and opened on a large hall down-
stairs, while there was a spacious drawing room
upstairs which had doors leading out on to veran-
das facing north and east. Very often there were
lavish parties at the Hall with excellent food and
wines. On one special occasion the entrée consisted
of a complete morocoy (land tortoise) for each
guest. A sort of miniature railway with two din-

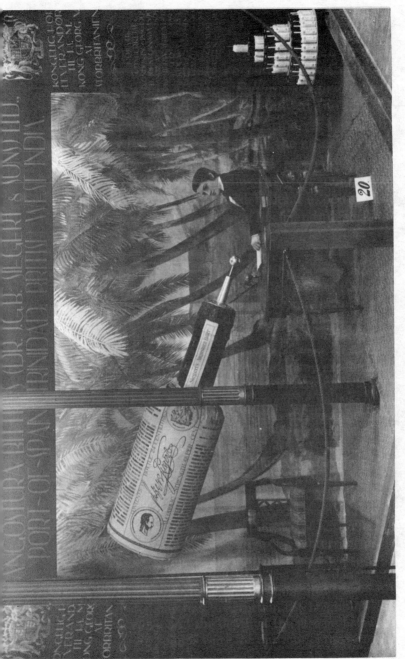

Siegert Booth at an International Exhibition in Germany.
The coconut trees give an exotic flavour.

Siegert's Premises, 3, 6 & 8 George Street, Trinidad, 1915.
Buggy's were still the usual mode of transport.

Bottling & packing Angostura Bitters, at George Street, 1910.
The supervisor is in the foreground.

The Sailing Ship "Doctor Siegert", built in 1875, and wrecked off Chacachacare twenty years later.

WITH THE BARK 'DR. SIEGERT' TO TRINIDAD.

An intrepid Translation of the German Account of the Wreck, 1895.

The bark "Dr Siegert" of the firm Franzius, Henschen & Co. Bremen, sailed to Port of Spain in the island of Trinidad, brought piece-goods there and returned to Bremen with a cargo of pitch, coconuts and Angostura Bitters, well-known as the best remedy for stomach-disorders and sufferings from dysentery. This "good drop" was manufactured in Doctor Siegert's Establishment on the Orinoco, made out of the bark of the Galipea.

The ship arrived after an average-travelling time of 58 days on May 13th, 1895 at the docks of Port of Spain. There the unloading started immediately and new freight was taken on board subsequently, Pitch in barrels, coconuts and cases with Angostura Bitters. Furthermore came two passengers aboard for the crossing to Bremen.

The Bark lay ready to sail at the end of June for the voyage homewards, waiting for a favourable sailing wind. Unfortunately the so very much desired wind did not set in.... Finally, on July 4th towards mid-day, a moderate easterly breeze set in and the Captain tried to gain by force with full sails the thoroughfare at Boca Grande. But luck was not favourable to the ship, they did not succeed to get in the open sea. Shortly before the destination near the dangerous Diamond Rock, the wind abate and the Bark drove in the strong current towards the land.

Captain Wilms gave immediate orders to drop anchor. Whilst carrying out the manoeuvring with the anchor, there was a delay in the falling of the anchors caused by the capstan becoming indistinctable. A few minutes were lost which were enough to determine the fate of the ship. After the obstacle was removed the ship ran aground on the rocky ground.

After the sails were brailed up the Captain immediately let a boat hoist out and both passenger as well as the captain's wife and children were rowed ashore not to have them exposed to danger.

According to measurings in the hold, the Bark collected at first only little water, but towards evening the water in the hold increased quickly. Once more the Captain sent a boat ashore to get workmen to assist the crew with pumping....

A tug-boat was ordered to take the bark in tow, which brought salvage materials along, moreover a steam pump also. The ship was now brought in shallow waters and carefully put down. A last effort was yet made with the steam-pump to get the water out of the hold. Thirty hours continuously was the steam pump in operation, but this also did not bring the result as desired.

A diver examined the ship's bottom on July 6th, to caulk the leak under water. Hereby it turned out that the ship was aground with the leak on a rock therefore the diver could not accomplish anything. The "Doctor Siegert" had to be relinquished. They still succeeded however, to save 2000 barrels with pitch, the greatest part of the Angostura Bitters and the coconuts. The ship's sails and rigging system exclusively, was sold for $705.00

"The Hall", Chancery Lane, home of Carlos Damaso Siegert, previously (till 1886) the property of Charles William Warner.

ner-wagons transported the food from the kitchen
to the dining room. The Siegert family received
their relatives and friends every Monday evening.
The gentlemen would gather on the veranda, and
the ladies sat around in the drawing room where
there was a lovely grand piano which was played
by the young ladies of the family. The major part
of the house was destroyed by fire in 1920, shortly
after it had been sold by the Siegert family, (who
had occupied it for 34 years) and it is at present
the site of Bishop Anstey High School.

Don Carlos was a bit of an eccentric, one of
his peculiarities being that when he took a fancy
to a particular piece of furniture or china, he always bought three of the type, one for himself and
two for his brothers. These were not gifts as (being the senior partner) he would charge his brothers' accounts in the firm with their cost. For instance, the standing altar lamp with filigree metal
at the top, in the Archbishop's chapel was a gift
from Alfredo Siegert (via purchase by Carlos!) to
the then Fr. Dowling (subsequently Archbishop)
two similar lamps being in the possession of the
family!

Don Carlos was a ruthless businessman
and domineering in his management of the company. The peculiar form of the Company deed was:
"Carlos D. Siegert, or in his absence etc. Alfredo
C. Siegert or in his absence etc. Luis B.C. Siegert
etc." In the 1890's he had a very serious quarrel
with his brother Luis and while the enmity lasted,
reduced the sum Luis was empowered to draw
from the business, to $150 a month. Happily, the

two brothers were eventually reconciled.

The oldest Siegert was a meticulous man, always neat and impeccably dressed. He had a horror of disorder and was most fastidious about hygiene, and so it resulted that children who inevitably were noisy and grubby or at least had sticky fingers were not his favourite companions. Consequently he devised a ritual appearance for his many grandchildren and great-nieces and nephews. On a Sunday morning he would seat himself in his large chair at one end of the very spacious drawing room of the Hall, and the children would be lined up at the entrance to the room and would be directed forwards one at a time towards him. He would cast a loving look on the child and graciously dispense to it a half-crown. The child would then walk around his chair and depart the room from a back exit. This is the memory all kept of him - the Sunday ritual and present and then the swift departure out of the presence!

Don Carlos was a highly sensitive man. He had a slight cast to one eye - a squint - and he was extremely touchy about it. One day he went in his carriage followed by a number of his carts, to a wholesale provision merchant in Port of Spain, by the name of Ortiz. He ordered a substantial quantity of goods from Ortiz and these were duly loaded onto the carts lined up behind his carriage. Ortiz, on saying goodbye, seemed to have noticed for the first time that there was something wrong with Carlos' eye and said to him. *"Pero, Don Carlos tu tienes algo en el ojo"* (But Don Carlos, you have something in your eye). At which point, Don Carlos said to Ortiz, "You think I have something in my eye do you. Take all these goods off my carts". This was done immediately and Don Carlos left in high dudgeon, to return to the Hall.

On October 10th 1903 Carlos Siegert died of congestion of the lungs after a very short illness, indeed up to a few days before his death having gone as was customary to his place of business at his usual hour of 7.00 a.m. His death was followed within eighteen months by that of his brother Luis.

Luis was the youngest of the three brothers who came from Venezuela. When the brothers moved to Trinidad he became a partner in the firm. His marriage to Camilla Chipchase was without issue and the couple adopted Viola de Krani. Luis was a very kind man and a pillar of the Roman Catholic Church. He was greatly esteemed by the employees of his firm for his never failing kindness and consideration and his domestic staff were devoted to him as a friend as well as a master. But he had one terrible weakness which was a common failing of the family. He could not resist good food and as a result, he and many others in the family exhibited a very portly look.

Luis had financed the formation of the Union Club and held a mortgage on the Club in lieu of the finance he provided. Quite naturally he was very fond of the establishment and frequented it, to dine and play poker with his friends. The story is told that on one particular Corpus Christi, it was planned that after the procession a

number of the members would go to the Club for
lunch, and with this in view, four dozen special
pastelles were prepared. For some reason, Luis
left the procession very early and finding himself
at the Club decided to sample the pastelles, four
at a time. They were absolutely delicious, worthy
indeed to constitute a meal in themselves! When
Luis placed his thirteenth order for four pastelles,
he was told regretfully that he had consumed the
Club's whole stock, and the Club had then to apologize to the hot, exhausted and hungry patrons who
arrived after the end of the procession!   One
Christmas, when the family foolishly left Luis in
a side room to carve the ham and two turkeys, he
sheepishly entered the dining room some time
later and confessed that he had regretably eaten
as fast as he carved and that now only one turkey
was left. He was however such a kind and lovable
character that he was readily forgiven.

Apart from being a member of the Cham-
ber of Commerce Luis was not active in public life.
He died of double pneumonia after a short illness
on the 1st June 1905, at his residence 8 Queen's
Park West (Stanmore Avenue). As might be expected, the Roman Catholic Archbishop presided
at his funeral, but interestingly enough Captain
Jansen and the officers of the visiting German
Gunboat *Panther* were also in the cortege, - and
this was the reason why. A few days before his
death, Captain Jansen and the officers had hosted
a sumptuous luncheon for Luis on board the *Panther* which was anchored some way off shore in
the stream. After a huge meal, while Luis was

being rowed back to shore he was drenched in a thunderstorm, resulting in his contracting pneumonia.

The lists of mourners at the funerals of the Siegert brothers are of interest as they show how the Siegerts were integrated into the French creole society (as also the English) possibly because of their Roman Catholic religion and Spanish antecedents from Venezuela. At Alfredo's funeral for instance there were to be the widest possible range of upper middle class society, including the following names:

German: Von Weiller, Schack, Boos, Monch, Gerold.
Old Spanish: Farfan, Sorzano, Caracciolo.
Venezuelan: Prada, Betancourt, Llanos.
Portuguese: Ribeiro, Pereira.
Irish & Corsican: Kernahan, Costelloe, Laughlin, Orsini, Calvini.
French Creole: Maingot, de Lapeyrouse, Leotaud, Pollonais, de Gannes.
Scottish and British: Warner, Bushe, Rust, Fraser, Scot, Gordon Gordon.
And a number of persons from prominent coloured families.

After the death of her dearly beloved husband, Camilla not having children of her own had nothing to live for and died a few months after Louis. She was buried near to him in the Lapeyrouse cemetery in the spacious Siegert vault, graced by a bust of Dr.J.G.B. Siegert sculpted by the famous Venezuelan Sculptor, Palacio.

On Luis' death, Alfredo Cornelio Siegert remained sole owner of the Angostura Bitters formula and of the firm. He admitted into partnership his son, Alfredo Galo, and his two nephews (the sons of Carlos) George and Albert. The shares of the partnership were Alfredo Cornelio 85%, Alfredo Galo, George and Albert 5% each. In 1909 Alfredo formed a public company in London (still owned entirely by the family) with the name of *Angostura Bitters (Dr. J.G.B. Siegert & Sons) Limited*.

Considerable profits from the Bitters were used to acquire large landholdings in Trinidad, and the sale of these brought larger profits. On 5th May 1904 the newspapers reported: "The Town Commissioners have purchased a site for a new cemetery for £3,194. It is Mr. Siegert's "Terre Brulée", 49 acres in extent; it is situated on the road to Four Roads, just east of Fort George Hill." Up to 1899 Woodbrook estate, 367 acres once under sugar and within one mile of the town of Port of Spain, was owned by the firm of W.F.Burnley & Co. of Glasgow. This firm went into liquidation and the estate was bought by the Siegert family for the sum of £50,000. A housing development scheme was undertaken, under the direction of George McAllister-Boyack. The estate was then laid out in lots for sale or lease to form a settlement constituting the modern Woodbrook. The connection of the estate with the Siegert family was preserved in the names of the various streets of Woodbrook named after the members of the family: Cornelio, Carlos, Alfredo, Luis, Alberto,

Christmas in "The Hall", with a 'real' Christmas tree,
a Crèche, Christmas presents, the piano for playing Carols.

Carlos Damaso Siegert, 1830- 1903.
This photo was taken in Germany in 1900.

Ana Apolonia Siegert (née Grillet) his wife.

Alfredo Cornelio Siegert, 1847-1919.
The second of the three brothers who came to Trinidad.

Luis Benjamin Siegert, 1853-1905.
The youngest brother.

The Siegert ladies in their carriage round the Savannah.
The band played in the bandstand every Sunday afternoon.
The lovely lace was very much favoured by Venezuelan ladies.

The Siegert children (at right) in the Governor's Gardens.
Note the nanny. In 1890, the full dress was *de rigeur* for all.

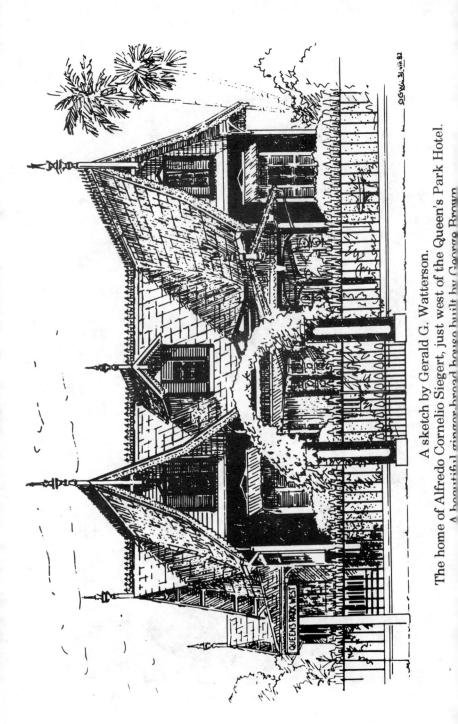

A sketch by Gerald G. Watterson.

The home of Alfredo Cornelio Siegert, just west of the Queen's Park Hotel.

A beautiful gingerbread house built by George Brown

Rosalino, Anna, Petra and Gallus. There is also a square opposite St. Crispin's Anglican Church which is known as Siegert's Square and which was the site of the old sugar factory. In January 1911 the Siegert family decided to sell the developed estate and offered it first to Government. Negotiations followed and eventually 348 acres were sold to the Town Board for £85,000, and restrictions were imposed with respect to tenancy, which resulted in it acquiring a middle-class character.

A very large acreage of land was bought also by the family in the Chaguaramas and Carenage area (the reason for which we will see later) and on Monos and Gaspar Grande where holiday homes were built. The Siegert family in fact helped to popularize 'the islands' as a holiday resort, through their properties at BelleVue, Gasparee and Siegert's Point, Marielva, on Monos. The 'islands' were indeed the focus of the Siegerts' family life. Friends and family meant everything to them and they enjoyed themselves together as a group, oftentimes three generations of them!

When the First World War began in 1914, to ensure that they were not associated with the German enemy, the Siegerts christened the large bay near to their Monos property, 'Allies Bay'. However, the world war was to be an unmitigated disaster for the Siegert family, for the sales of Angostura Bitters plunged dramatically, and worse again, Alfredo had overextended himself in some very (at that time) unwise investments. He had never settled the debts to the estates of his late brothers by giving them any shares in the new

public company. Instead, he heavily financed
Eugene Andre in the construction and operation
of a lime juice factory and a factory for the production of starch from cassava, both of which
failed.

In addition, in 1890 he had submitted a
proposal to Government for establishing a railway
on the seaboard from Port of Spain to
Chaguaramas where he planned to construct large
and commodious docks with quays, warehouses,
coaling and other dock facilities. The scheme was
pronounced a most feasible one presenting few
engineering difficulties, and the advantages of the
Bay as an anchorage could not be overlooked. The
undertaking was estimated to cost some £500,000.
However, due to the opposition of the merchants
who owned and operated lighters in the Port of
Spain harbor, the scheme never materialized and
permission to build the railway was turned down
by the Colonial authorities. Instead of making a
fortune in the scheme (which was perhaps a wonderful idea born before its time) Alfredo was left
holding a lot of practically worthless land, and
more importantly, the £50,000 he had already
spent dredging the harbour was money down the
drain. The Angostura shares hit rock bottom and
as Alfredo was unable to settle his debts to the
estates of his brothers or to repay the loans, the
banks, Barclay's Bank and Gordon Grant & Co.,
eventually took over and sold all the assets which
they held as security, the Angostura shares being
bought up mainly in England. At his death in 1919
Alfred Cornelio possessed no assets, all his landed

properties having been sold to pay his debts.

Alfredo Cornelio had been the most colourful of the three Siegert brothers. He had been highly educated in Germany, was particularly good at figures and fluent in a number of languages, but had a most unassuming manner. He was a Director of Trinidad Fire Insurance Ltd. and of the Commercial Telephone Company. The Governor offered him a seat on the Legislative Council in 1904, but he declined accepting, giving as the reason that his business did not allow him to devote sufficient time to the Council. Alfredo Cornelio had lived in a beautifull ginger-bread house built by George Brown, next to the Queen's Park Hotel. His brother Luis (as we have seen) had also occupied a residence facing the Queen's Park Savannah, for as the Mirror of 4th April 1903 put it:

> All who can possibly afford it live out of the town in a quarter called the Savannah, a wide level plain, round which are many charming villas, light, airy wooden structures, with pretty balconies in front and shady gardens all round. The Savannah itself is a large park where (horse) races are held and cricket and other games are played. On the one side of the Park is the chief Hotel, on the other side the Governor's residence and the grounds surrounding which are open to the public. Here a band plays twice a week and the rank and fashion of the place congregate. It is interesting at such times to see the coloured people dressed in the latest Parisian fashions eyeing one another in the most approved European style.

After the death of Carlos, Alfredo Cornelio transferred his residence to the Hall, and soon became one of the most prominent race-horse owners, - possessing a great creole named Mayette. At the time of his brother's death, a complete inventory of the furniture etc in the Hall was taken and makes interesting reading. Here are some extracts.

In store rooms 1 - 6

30 doz. Spanish wines	$120	2 cases mineral water	$10
3 cases fine Champagne	$98	5 cases H.M. Water	$20
4 cases Siegert Bouquet	$24	73 case Florida Water	$292
5 cases Bitters	$5	18 cases whisky	$180
400 doz. claret	$960	19 cases Port wine	$190
1 case Champagne	$24	8 dozen claret	$24
2 cases gin	$15	6 cases beer	$42
1 lot Spanish wines and liqueurs			$100

The main drawing room

1 Grand Piano	$360	1 marble-top table	$100
1 Stand lamp	$15	1 music stand	$4.50
2 Consoles	$120	2 bent. Rockers	$10
1 Suite Mahogany:			
Sofa, 7 chairs, 2 arm chairs, 1 table			$70
1 metal table	$5	2 Rockers	$20
1 mable top table	$6	1 carpet	$5
2 sofas, 2 arm chairs	$50	1 what. bamboo	$5
2 Rockers	$25	1 occas.table	.75c
1 stand lamp	$5	1 metal table	$5
1 flower stand	$1	1 stand	$1
1 bamboo stand	$1.50	1 flower stand	.60c
1 lot vases and ornaments			$25

Alfredo Galo (son of Alfredo Cornelio) and his dog.
Like all the Siegerts, a large man, impeccably dressed.

Siegert's Bay - Marielva - on the S.E. Point of Monos. The Siegerts popularised holidays 'down the islands'.

Swimming at Marielva to the sound of sweet music!
Friends and family-life meant everything to the Siegerts.

An expedition to the Blue Grotto (caves) of Gasparee. All seem to be utterly exhausted - except the dog!

Outing to Copperhole Monos, 8-5-1898.
arranged by Luis B.C.Siegert - for businessmen & lawyers!
Back Row: L. to R. Johnnie Wehekind, F.E.Scott, Harry Vincent, Max Leotaud,
Sir Henry Alcazar, Jean Guiseppi, Eddie Scott.
Middle Row: S.Austin, Aucher Warner, Tico Coryat, Frank Farfan, Willy Kernahan,
Edgar Agostini, Ellis Grell.
Seated: Thor Schjolseth, Carlos Siegert, Charlie Leotaud, Luis Siegert, Léon Wehekind.

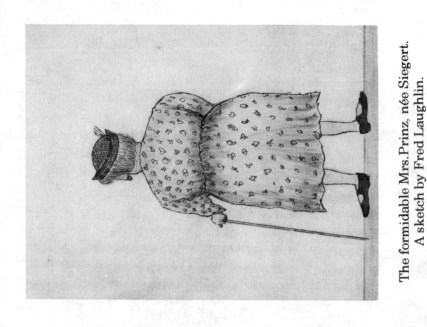

Luis Siegert playing poker.
One of 20 sketches in a framed montage
hung in the Union Club.

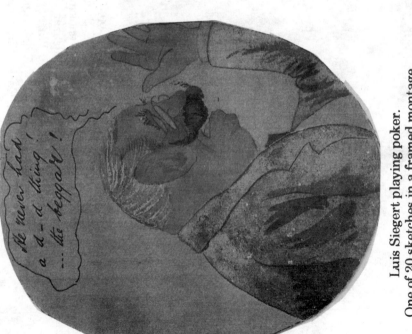

The formidable Mrs. Prinz, née Siegert.
A sketch by Fred Laughlin.

Visitors Room No.2

2 single iron bedsteads		1 table	$2.50
and springs	$20	1 walnut press	$20
Washstand	$1.20	2 B.W.Chairs	$1.50
1 hatstand	$4.50	1 night chair	$10
1 towel rack	.60c	1 wicker table	.60c
1 clothes basket	.50c	1 Bidet	$1.20
1 step ladder	.60c	1 night pillar	$1.50

In 1921 Pointz Mackenzie bought all the Angostura shares he could acquire and gained full control of the Company but within a few years he got into financial trouble and sold out his full Angostura shareholding, the shares becoming widely dispersed. Meanwhile, Alfredo Galo Siegert, the son of Alfredo Cornelio, continued on as managing director of the firm and was the only one to possess the secret formula. He retired from the Managing Directorship in 1954, and his son Robert succeeded him as Managing Director. Up to 1947 the formula for Angostura Bitters was a closely guarded secret, which was so carefully kept by the partners, that they personally did all the work of compounding the article and only the work of filling bottles and packing cases was done by the employees; but in that year, one of the Directors, A.C.Gomez, was entrusted with the formula which is at present tucked away at a Bank in New York, as safe as money can make it!

In 1958 the Trinidad Government bought out the controlling interest in the Company in order to prevent it being acquired by a Canadian businessman who had made a take-over bid intending, if successful, to move the Company to tax-free Bermuda. The Government then resold the controlling interest to a private company called *Siegert Holdings Limited*, on terms which ensured that the manufacture of Angostura Bitters would remain permanently in Trinidad. All the shareholders of Siegert Holdings Ltd. were employees of the Company and their families. Alfredo Galo Siegert, the grandson and Robert W. Siegert the great-grandson of the founder, held between them the controlling interest in Siegert Holdings Ltd, so that the full control of the Angostura Company which was lost by the Siegert family in 1918, was regained by the Siegert family forty years later. And since then the Company has gone from one success to another.

Production of Angostura Bitters is at present about 140,000 cases a year but it is now only a part of the Angostura business concern. As early as 1936, Robert Siegert successfully lobbied for the establishment of a chemical control and research laboratory, and Angostura was successfully launched on an extensive diversification program. The firm currently produces, Angos Gin, Molotov Vodka, Mokatika Coffee Liqueur and most important of all, the well known Royal Oak Rum and White Oak, and most recently Angostura Premium White, which are, like the bitters, exported all over the world. Last year, with sales of over $240 million dollars, Angostura gave the Government in various duties and taxes over 100 million dollars, so that the Angostura Staff members sometimes refer to themselves as semi-government employees!

At present, John Gordon Siegert, (the son of Robert,) who retired from the Board of Angostura in 1990, his two children and cousin Janel (See family tree on page 147) are the only descendants of Dr. J.G.B. Siegert (through his second wife) who still carry his name, a name which through Angostura Biters is indelibly etched in Trinidad's history and is a source of pride to the people of the nation, - where indeed the name Siegert has now become almost synonymous with success.

Chapter 5

The Boos Family

If you would go up high, then use your own legs!
Do not get yourselves carried aloft; do not seat
yourselves on other peoples backs or heads!
                          Friedrich Wilhelm Nietzsche.

The Boos family, like the Urichs, came from Hesse-Darmstadt. Karl Boos was very much in love with Johanna Spiess, but he was only 19 and she 20. Even though the families of the young people looked kindly on the friendship, Karl had to leave the beautiful little town of Meerholtz in Hesse to go out to seek his fortune in far away Trinidad, in the West Indies. Karl's mother's people were school teachers and ministers of the Lutheran Church and on his father's side the family owned a business where leather goods were made and sold. Conceivably, after he had acquired experience in Trinidad and his father was old enough to retire, he might come back to take over the business. In the meantime, he could join the other young people from the neighbouring towns who were already working in Trinidad as merchants' clerks and agents, in Port of Spain, the capital of the island. And so, in 1873, when he was twenty years old, Karl sailed to Trinidad to work as a clerk for Fritz Zurcher who operated a number of concerns in the island.

A clerk in those days meant a sales clerk or shop assistant, responsible for dealing with the customers and keeping the stock in order. It was then customary to place a private mark upon an article for sale indicating the price, and the clerk was allowed and expected to get as much as he could from the customer, above the figure named. The young Germans did not have an easy time. Here is a description (given in 1888) of a clerk routed by a "Cheups" given by a lady (as creole women were invariably known.)

> A lady goes into a dry goods store and points to something.
> Lady: "How you does sell dis?"
> Clerk: "Sixty cents Madame, best quality."
> Lady: "Eh, eh! You's tink me foolish?"
> Clerk: "Well, I'll give it you for half a dollar."
> Lady: Without condescending a reply, *sucks her teeth*, (a most impressive form of speech which means volumes - extreme disgust, withering contempt etc), wheels round and proceeds to leave the store with much dignity - when nearing the street -
> Clerk: Here Madame, take it for four bits.

However, Karl was able to adapt to his new circumstances and worked efficiently and happily for three years with Zurcher, and after that they parted amicably when the fortunes of young Boos became entwined with those of an extremely wealthy New Yorker named Hancox who offered him a position as clerk in the firm of Harriman. This is how matters came to pass.

In 1867, Hancox, under the protection of

the American flag set up regular steam communication between Port of Spain and Ciudad Bolivar.
At first everything went happily for him. His business prospered and his daughter Josephine married the very eligible Georg Wuppermann, a pros-
perous merchant of Trinidad. But in August 1871
there was in Venezuela a rising of revolutionaries
known as 'the Blues'. The 'Hero' one of the steamers of Hancox's line was seized at Guyana la Vieja
(where hundreds of years before, young Raleigh
had been killed searching for El Dorado), the
United States flag was hauled down, the captain
imprisoned and the steamship used as a man-of-
war and transport for troops. Worse was to come.
The revolutionaries having seized the 'Hero', the
Government in turn promptly took possession of
Hancox's other ship, the 'Nurias', deposed her captain, and against his protest manned and armed
her and engaged her in a most destructive naval
combat with her sister ship the 'Hero'.

Moreover, partly as a result of this revolu-
tion, in 1872 the House of Gerold and Urich, hardware and provision merchants in Trinidad, failed,
Georg Wuppermann being then one of the partners. So Hancox, in addition to his heavy financial losses, was now left with a bankrupt son-in-
law. Josephine's sister, Elizabeth, was the wife
of John Neilson Harriman. Old man Hancox, attempting to recoup his family's fortunes, advanced
a sum of money to his son-in- law, John Neilson
Harriman, "being desirous of making provision for
his daughter Josephine, to be invested in establishing the business of commission merchant in

Port of Spain under the name of J.N.Harriman
and Company, but in trust for the separate use
and benefit of the said Josephine Wuppermann".
Unfortunately, Elizabeth Harriman died in Port
of Spain within a year and her husband returned
to the United States some short time later. Georg
Wuppermann was then left to run the firm which
became the sole agent in the West Indies for Angostura Bitters, (which moved to Trinidad in
1875.) Carlos D.Siegert, the owner of Angostura,
became good friends with Georg and was the godfather of his son.

　　　As a clerk in the firm of Harriman, with
good prospects of advancement, in 1876 Karl Boos
brought out from Germany his future wife
Johanna Spiess. They were married in the Anglican Church from the Zurcher home, known as Blarney (and later as Ellerslie when it was bought by
the Rapseys), just outside of Port of Spain.

　　　In 1878 Siegert's offered their New York
agency to Georg Wupperman who then left with
his wife Josephine for the United States. Before
leaving, Josephine Wupperman drew up a memo-
randum of agreement between herself and Karl
Boos, making him Head Clerk in the firm of
J.N.Harriman and Co., for three years, during
which time he was not to engage in any other business and was to render quarterly accounts. This
agreement was extended for a further three years
in 1882. In 1885 the Company was purchased by
Dr.J.G.B. Siegert and Sons, and it must have been
a matter of weeks later that the Siegerts sold it
(at a good profit) to Karl Boos, according to a re-

port written by him: "By deed of January 23rd, 1885, I bought from Dr J.G.B. Siegert and Sons, the business and good will of J.N.Harriman and Co. Port of Spain, who had acted as agents of the said Siegert and Sons for the sale on commission of the Bitters and other Cordials manufactured by them."

It is clear from these transactions (and others already mentioned) that the German merchants in Trinidad (and to a lesser extent the Corsican) formed a loose economic union with one another, perhaps a little like the Syrians at present. They were willing to assist their fellow Germans who were in difficulty and when businesses were sold they frequently passed from the hands of one German merchant to another. For instance, a deed of the 6th June 1887 attempting to simplify the business of Wuppermann and Prahl, lists the following who had interests in the firm: Duncan Campbell, Karl Boos, Frederick Urich, William Cunningham, E.J.Wainwright, Adolfo Wuppermann, Fritz Zurcher, Fritz Prahl, Charles Marc Vessiny, Paul Vessiny, Eugene Cipriani, Joseph Pollonais, Eugène Wehekind.

The German merchants at this time were both owners and managers of their firms. They worked alongside the employees and much harder and longer (sometimes from 7 a.m. to 6 p.m) than any of them. Their office was not separated off entirely from the main store. They were here there and everywhere, looking after sales, chatting with customers, directing operations, sometimes necessarily with the use of language unsuited to the delicate ears of children.

A piece of advice that could have profitably been given to some of the merchants (though not necessarily to Boos) was: "The strong man never makes a bad debt nor a good friend. He is a real worker and ends up with enough money to buy all the things he is incapable of enjoying. Strength is admirable but it needs to be diluted with human weakness before it is fit for human consumption".

And conditions of work were not pleasant. Besides the dust and heat, stores in lower Port of Spain, like Harriman's (which was at 2 South Quay till 1896) were too close to sea-level to avail of the sewers laid down in the town in the 1890's. So that presumably sanitary arrangements at Harriman's were somewhat similar to those described at a neighbouring store.

> The firm was at sea level. Our sanitary arrangements consisted of a large tin at the side of which was a large box containing coal dust. On the wall was a notice which read: "Please use plenty of coal dust from the box". One morning was found a red cross drawn across the notice and a patois transcription which said "Fai comme chat", meaning "do as the cat does". The notice remained there for many years before the sewering was completed.

Carl Siegert had imposed very harsh conditions on Karl Boos when he acquired Harriman's. The firm's assets had been tabled as $56,757.26 and this was named for the purchase price of the business. No money was paid immediately but interest on the purchase price or on such balance as might remain was to be 15%, and for the purchase of goodwill Boos had agreed to pay an annuity of $2,000 for 20 years. To prevent Boos borrowing money at a lower interest rate and paying off Siegert, by the terms of the agreement, no partner was to be taken into the firm nor a loan obtained. But by hard work and expanding the sale of cocoa and Bitters, Boos soon paid off the money. Siegert told him: "I never expected you would pay us so soon; in this way what is our profit?"

Karl Boos and his wife, Johanna, were a very happy couple and they had five sons and two daughters. The sons were all educated in Germany, for Karl's growing business success kept pace with his expanding family. In 1883, on the newly developed Tranquillity lands, where lots were sold by the Government at auction with a lease of 199 years, he had erected a magnificent family home, of imported yellow bricks and concrete, with well-cured pitch pine timbers and floors, on lots then numbered as 34-36 Tranquillity Boulevard. Said to have been designed and built by the Scottish Architect, George Brown, in the early Art Nouveau style, the house can be described as a gem of Creole Architecture. The design is quite original in that the house is raised high off the ground, the floor height is almost doubled to create a *piano nobile*; elongated and slender posts uphold the roof and there are galleries on both floors. The roof seems to sail over the open galleries and there is a distinct and definite articulation between it and the façade, penetrated as it is by two dormers with a box-like lantern-like structure in the centre, giving the suggestion and feeling of Imperial India.

From the front gallery of the house, a view could be had of the harbour of Port of Spain and of the beautiful hills of the Northern Range. There was a private gas plant to light the house, the gas pipes leading down to the chandeliers (and later, being used as conduits for the electric wire, when electricity was introduced into Port of Spain). Karl filled the house with the ornate, ersatz antique furniture then being mass-produced in Germany, and with expensive and truly beautiful china and silver. In the yard, there was a large semi-underground area to store ice. To date, 110 years after its construction, the house is still in good condition, having been occupied by the Boos family up to last year.

Karl kept no stables, for the house though cool and with a spacious garden and on the very edge of the town, was close enough to his business place for him to walk there every morning to begin his long and hard day's work - sometimes early enough to see the water-carts sprinkling water on the streets to keep down the dust in the dry season. According to *The Mirror*:

> The day begins with a light breakfast at 6, then people go away to business which begins at 7.00. At 11 there is a *déjeuner à la fourchette*, tea at 4 and a heavy dinner at 7 or 8.

Karl was an enterprising businessman. In 1884 the telephone had been introduced into Trinidad by W. Gray, for the Tropical American

Company of New York. In 1885 it was taken over by a locally formed firm, the Commercial Telephone Company Ltd. Karl Boos, the first chairman, took a lively interest in the concern, and to him was due in great measure the success of the company. It was reported that: "All the Government institutions of the city were (by 1886) in telephonic communication with the Exchange and scarcely any complaints are ever made in any direction of the service. The operators (ladies) are polite and careful", - and hopefully, did not listen in to too many conversations!

In 1896 Harriman and Co. moved from their original premises at 2 South Quay , to their present location at 61 Marine (now Independence) Square. More and more they entered into the cocoa shipping business; for world consumption of cocoa (produced mainly from the West Indies and South America) had increased from 20,000 tons in 1850 to nearly 100,000 tons in 1900, with consumption in Germany increasing rapidly. As the French creoles in Trinidad built up production levels from 1870 onwards, it was to a considerable extent the German merchants in the capital who controlled the market, exporting cocoa and importing goods, mainly for the estates, though later, for sale to the population of Port of Spain.

In 1896 when he was age 19 and had completed his education in Germany, Carl August Boos had joined his father Karl, as cashier and in 1900, he was taken into partnership. His father then left with his wife (and some of the children) to settle in New York where he opened the firm of

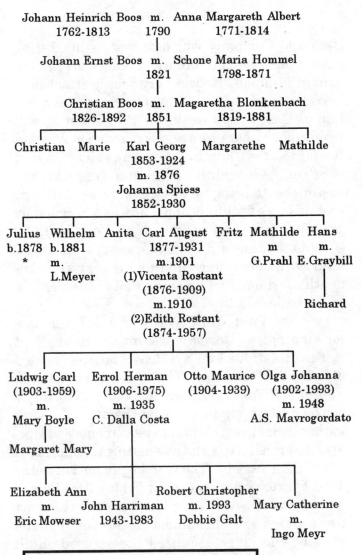

Johann Heinrich Boos m. Anna Margareth Albert
1762-1813   1790   1771-1814

Johann Ernst Boos m. Schone Maria Hommel
                   1821   1798-1871

Christian Boos m. Magaretha Blonkenbach
1826-1892   1851   1819-1881

Christian   Marie   Karl Georg   Margarethe   Mathilde
                    1853-1924
                    m. 1876
                    Johanna Spiess
                    1852-1930

Julius   Wilhelm   Anita   Carl August   Fritz   Mathilde   Hans
b.1878   b.1881   1877-1931   m   m.
  *   m.   m.1901   G.Prahl   E.Graybill
        L.Meyer   (1)Vicenta Rostant
                          (1876-1909)
                          m.1910   Richard
                        (2)Edith Rostant
                          (1874-1957)

Ludwig Carl   Errol Herman   Otto Maurice   Olga Johanna
(1903-1959)   (1906-1975)   (1904-1939)   (1902-1993)
   m.   m. 1935   m. 1948
Mary Boyle   C. Dalla Costa   A.S. Mavrogordato

Margaret Mary

Elizabeth Ann   Robert Christopher
   m.   John Harriman   m. 1993   Mary Catherine
Eric Mowser 1943-1983   Debbie Galt   m.
                                            Ingo Meyr

* For Descendants of Julius see page 191.

Boos and Company which served as marketing
agents there for Harriman's. Young Carl ran the
firm in Trinidad. He was very deeply attached to
his father and over a period of twenty years wrote
him at least once a week. In 1901 when he was
twenty-four years of age, Carl married Vicenta
Rostant at the Church of the Sacred Heart in Port
of Spain. As a condition of his marriage, Carl had
to promise to bring up any children as Catholics
and this was faithfully done. It was a very happy
marriage but on a visit to New York in 1909,
Vicenta died aged 33 years, leaving Carl a widower with four young children. A year after her
death, Carl married Vicenta's older sister, Edith,
in Barbados, on the 1st July.

The First World War was a difficult time
for all people of German descent in Trinidad but
it was disastrous for Carl Boos who was accused
of being a German spy. The case came to court in
February 1919, when Carl A. Boos was formally
charged "with intent to assist the enemy" - with
gathering information of ship movements and storage of war materials and attempting to supply coal
to German vessels. The case began on Thursday
13th February and ended on Friday 21st February, a total of seven days, and each day the court
proceedings were headlined in the newspapers.
Finally, the judge acquitted the accused on all
charges. The case was summed up as follows: "An
innocent man labouring under a disgraceful charge
meets it in a bold and straightforward manner and
takes the first opportunity which presents itself
of denying on oath the truth of the charge".

TRIAL OF CARL BOOS.

SENSATIONAL WITHDRAWAL BY CROWN PROSECUTOR.

CHARGE OF INTENT TO ASSIST ENEMY ABANDONED.

EXPLANATIONS BY ACCUSED CONSIDERED SATISFACTORY.

INDICTMENT CONFINED TO BREACH OF REGULATIONS.

THE case of Rex v Carl August Boos was resumed in the Hall of Justice yesterday, before His Honour Sir A. V. Lucie Smith, Kt., C.J. The attendance was similar to that of the preceding days,

THE APPEARANCES.

Sir Henry Alcazar, Kt., K.C., associated with Mr. L. A. P. O'Reilly and instructed by Messrs. J. D. Sellier & Co., appeared for the accused, while the Hon. Aucher Warner, B.A., K.C., Attorney-General, associated with Mr. William Savary and instructed by Mr. A. D. O'Connor, Crown Solicitor, appeared to prosecute.

THE CHARGES.

The charge was as follows :—

(1) That Carl August Boos at various times during the years 1914 to 1918 inclusive did without lawful authority attempt to elicit information with respect to the movements of ships of His Majesty or His Majesty's Allies with intent to assist the enemy contrary to Section 18 (1) of the Defence of the Colony (Consolidation) Regulations 1917.

(2) That Carl August Boos on the 14th and 16th days of August last did collect and attempt to elicit information from Lieutenant Henry Hamilton, the officer in charge of the Nelson Island Garrison Artillery, with respect to the storage of war material with intent to assist the enemy, contrary to Section 18 (1) of the Colony (Consolidation) Regulations, 1917.

(3) That Carl August Boos on the 14th and 16th days of August last did collect and attempt to elicit information from Lieutenant Henry Hamilton, the officer in charge of the Nelson Island Garrison Artillery, with respect to measures connected with or intended for the Defence of the Colony with intent to assist the enemy contrary to Section 18 (1) of the Defence of the Colony (Consolidation) Regulations, 1917.

(4) That Carl August Boos on the 14th and 16th days of August last did collect and attempt to elicit information from Lieutenant Henry Hamilton, the officer in charge of the Nelson Island Garrison Artillery, and sometime within the previous thereto did collect and attempt to elicit information from the said Lieutenant Henry Hamilton and Major Harold de Pass of such a nature as is calculated to be directly or indirectly useful to the enemy with intent to assist the enemy contrary to Section 18 (1) of the Defence of the Colony Regulations 1917.

ACCUSED IN THE BOX.

Carl August Boos, continuing his examination in chief to Mr. L. A. P. O'Reilly said :

In 1914 I may have taken the cannister to my house. It contained my own personal papers as insurance policies and deeds. I was born in Trinidad. I lived here until the age of eleven, then I went to school in Germany for about five or six years, and afterwards went to Paris for about a year. After I left Paris I came to Trinidad in 1895 and have lived here continuously since then. I returned to Germany in 1906, and to Europe (London) in 1914. I have heard it suggested that I served in the German Army. There is no truth in that. I was never called up for service and I did not consider myself liable for service.

A SCHOOLBOY'S LARK.

When I was spending my vacation I got to know a young man serving in the German Army. One day I put on his uniform and took my photograph in it. I did it more as a lark. My mother had one of those photographs. I gave her the negative. I was scolded for this action by my uncle. This is the only thing to which I could contribute the statement that I served in the German Army. I had a libel action against the "Port of-Spain Gazette" in 1914, after the outbreak of the war. My case was that damage was done to my firm through their suggestion that I had assisted in the coaling of German vessels at sea. The "Gazette" did not defend the action. They agreed to pay the sum of £25 and costs and to apologise. There is no truth in the suggestion that my firm assisted in coaling German vessels. Throughout the war my sentiments have been in favour of the Allies. I have all my interest here I have no interest in Germany. My interests here consist of realty and the business. One quarter of the interest in the firm of Harriman & Co. belongs to me and three-quarters to my father. My father has interest also in America in realty and business. I like Germany as a country, but I never liked the form of Government. My father is German born, but he has been away from Germany for over 40 years. He has lived here for 25 years and in America about 20 years. I have seen my father several times since the war and have discussed the war with him. He was against the policy of Germany. He said if the military party had taken such a hold on Germany then Germany was paying

For the defence, Sir Henry Alcazar K.C. was associated with L.A.P.O'Reilly assisted by Messrs. J.D.Sellier and Co. - so that not surprisingly, the legal fees amounted to $40,000. But though completely acquitted, the defendant was psychologically a broken man, especially as he knew that a prominent fellow merchant was behind the prosecution by the Crown. He wrote to his father on the 14th March 1919.

> My dear Papa,
> Many thanks for your letter... that my constitution did not break down is remarkable, I feared it every moment... Everything as far as the case is concerned is over now and thank God for it too, but what I went through nobody will ever know, nor can I describe it....... and how these happenings will affect the future of my children worries me a great deal too.

And even though the case ended in his favour, Harriman and Company lost a great deal of business - the Ford Agency as well as Leyland and Harrison Lines.

In 1921 in a most amicable settlement, Carl's partnership with his father was dissolved and Carl purchased his father's interest in the business. In 1922, in New York, Karl Boos suffered a stroke. His son Willie who had been working with him had left the firm shortly before this occurred, so the younger brother Fritz was left to direct the business, and in June, Carl going on holiday gave full power of attorney to Fritz who was thus left in full charge of both Boos and Co. and Harriman's. During the next three months

Karl Georg Boos 1853 - 1924.

Carl August Boos, 1877-1931, & his wife, Vicenta, née Rostant.

Olga Mavrogordato, née Boos, eldest child of Carl.

Boos family mansion at Cipriani Boulevard, built in 1883.

Fritz entered the New York Stock Market and bought heavily on margin, stocks in sugar and cocoa with funds from the two firms he controlled. Then the bottom fell out of the market. Boos and Co. lost over one million dollars and went into liquidation. On the 27th October 1924 Karl Boos died in New York at the age of 71 years, a broken and disappointed man who had seen the fruits of his life's work wiped out in a few months. Six years later, his loving wife Johanna followed him to the grave.

In the debacle Harriman's lost over $240,000, but managed to struggle on. By 1926, however, the firm was on the very verge of bankruptcy with total indebtedness to the Banks of $171,533, for which they eventually compromised in the amount of $86,818 and all promissory notes were endorsed or made by Paul Urich, who pledged his share of the Urich estates as security and thus saved the firm of Harriman. From then on the firm began to prosper again in spite of very many difficulties.

There were no children from Carl's second marriage, but Edith, who (unlike most step-mothers who are either over-indulgent or much too strict) proved to be a wonderfully kind and devoted and firm step-mother to his children, Otto, Errol, Ludwig Carl and Olga, the only girl and the eldest of the family. The children were all brought up at the family home in Cipriani Boulevard, (the name of the street having been changed from Tranquillity to Cipriani in honour of the Mayor of Port of Spain, Emmanuel Cipriani.) Edith Boos was later to be a loving grandmother but also quite strict. On one occasion when a granddaughter dropped the family cat from the top of the stairs, by way of a scientific experiment to see if it would land on its feet (it did!) she had the erring young-ster locked away for a while in the 'dark room', (the large cubby-hole under the stairs) to repent of her bad behaviour!

Carl's younger brother, Julius, married Audrey Hobson. The union resulted in nine chil-dren (about whom more later).

The island of Huevos has been associated with the Boos family for nearly three-quarters of a century. It is a little islet with an area of 84 acres, situated off the north-west tip of Trinidad, with the island of Monos to the east and Chacachacare to the west. While stern cliffs face the north and the restless Caribbean sea, a broad sandy beach looks to the south and the calm wa-ters of the Gulf of Paria. The island was chris-tened by Columbus, El Delfin, (the Dolphin) per-haps because when seen from westward it looked like a dolphin; but the Spanish settlers called it Huevos (Eggs) because the Hawks Bill turtles used to come up in large numbers on the beach to lay their eggs. Fortunately, because it is a privately owned island, and with the help of occasional vis-its from the Coast Guard, the turtles once nearly wiped out, are returning in increasing numbers.

The island is also famous for its Oil Birds. In a large cave, the entrance of which is almost hidden from the sea, is a colony of Guacharo birds, *Steatornis caripensis*, the so called Diablotins, or little devils. This is a gregarious species, living and breeding in dark or pitch-black caves during the day and coming out at night to feed on fruit, mainly the seeds of palms. In flight it makes a series of clicks and chucks and navigates in the dark by echo-location. Its wingspread is three and a half feet, its plumage rich brown in colour with white spots. Its young grow very slowly flying only four months after hatching. During this time they become very fat and were collected by the Amerindians at the peak of their fatness and boiled down to produce oil for cooking and lighting. In a book by W.T.Hornaday, called *A Wild Animal Round-up*, published in 1925, there is a chapter on *Hunting the Cavebird in Trinidad* (1900) which describes entering the Huevos cave by boat and seeing about 200 birds there.

In 1900 Huevos was owned by 'Johnny' Wehekind, a keen fisherman. The fishing banks of Huevos were numerous and fish were plentiful. The most famous banks were, the Colonial Bank, Balata and Gran' Tante. In 1927 the island was leased to Carl   Boos and it has remained in the possession of the family ever since. One or two fishermen live on the island and act as caretakers for the low, wide-galleried owner's house, built just a few feet from the sea-shore. Three generations of the Boos family have enjoyed the fishing, the seining in the broad bay for cavalli, the swimming, and the friendly parties, over the years. In particular it was a great place for children.

In the early twentieth century, large parties used to be invited down the islands, for in-

stance the Schoeners organized a magnificent outing from the Thursday before Good Friday to Easter Monday, 1906, on Grells boat 'Banshee' to
Herrera's Bay (now St. Madeleine's Bay) at
Gasparee - though unfortunately Mrs. Goellnicht
broke her ankle on the Monday. And the Boos'
hospitality at Huevos was renowned far and wide.
A description of the 'islands' in a local newspaper
a few years after the turn of the century gives an
idea of the enjoyment.

> You can fish, you can swim, there is no reason
> why you should not shoot, dancing is not prohib-
> ited, cricket (bat and ball) is possible here and
> there, water polo is in the right element, card
> playing is an easy means of passing time (and
> incidentally cash) away, and in fact but for horse
> riding and driving one can indulge in practically
> all the forms of amusement one desires with the
> added particular ones of the Islands.

In 1935 the Duke and Duchess of Kent, at
the invitation of the Boos family, spent a day at
Huevos. Princess Margaret was there in 1958.
The British *Daily Mail* reported:

> Princess Margaret slipped away to a penny-sized
> tropical island today, to swim, sunbathe, and
> enjoy a beach picnic of iced champagne, cold
> salmon and chicken.

These were among the many distinguished
visitors whose names are signed on a linen table-
cloth embroidered with a map of the island of
Huevos. Very often, Olga Boos would look after
the visitors. As a kind hostess she allowed all who

wished to do so, to sign the table cloth, but as an
efficient and forceful historian and sometimes as
a person of strong likes and dislikes, and in order
to leave space for the signatures of subsequent and
more distinguished guests, she later carefully
erased all the signatures of those whom she chose
to classify as 'camp followers'!

Olga, in her younger days, had composed
and embroidered a beautiful little message
adorned with comic sketches in cross-stitch, which
she arranged to have framed and hung in the liv-
ing-room at Huevos. It ran as follows:

> GUESTS you are welcome here.
> Be at your ease.
> Get up when you're ready;
> Go to bed when you please.
>
> Happy to share with you,
> Such as we've got,
> The leaks in the roof,
> The soup in the pot.
>
> You don't have to thank us,
> Or laugh at our jokes.
> Sit deep and come often.
> You're one of the folks.

Many guests were entertained with the romantic tale of the shipwrecked Spanish galleon:

The fishermen will tell you that there is a submerged group of rocks abreast of the break in
Huevos Island, known as Boca Sin Entrada. Tradition has it that on calm moonlit nights you can
hear the sound of a chapel bell and the solemn

singing of ancient Latin hymns. Centuries ago,
they say, a Spanish Galleon was wrecked there
sailing into the Boca de Huevos. The ship carried a prince, and his chaplain summoned the
little choir boys to beg God for deliverance from
the awful peril.

There is indeed a record of a Spanish Galleon foundered in Trinidad waters on the 27th July
1666. It is believed to have struck a submerged
rock in the Gulf of Paria "some ten miles north of
Punta del Arenal" (Icacos Point). Perhaps this ship
was sailing out of the Boca and when the wind
failed was carried by the current on to the rocks.

The rare orchid, *Cyrtopodium Punctatum*,
with its beautiful four-foot spike of red and brown
flowers, and found only on Chacachacare and
Huevos, has been transplanted from the islet to
the family home in Cipriani Boulevard. Herman
Boos, Carl's son, who was an indefatigable worker
in building up the firm of Harriman, used to renew his strength on the weekends at Huevos. He
also became the President of the Island Owners'
Association, a group of proprietors of holiday
homes in the area. His sister Olga wrote a poem
full of feeling for the island that was so dear to
her.

Give me the sea and bright blue sky
And the beach where the turtles come,
The majestic hill and the simple house
And a swim in the brilliant sun -
Where all is peace and free from care
And the warmth of friendships glows.

Presentation of Medal of Merit, Gold, to Robert Boos,
by Sir Solomon Hochoy, on Independence Day 1972.

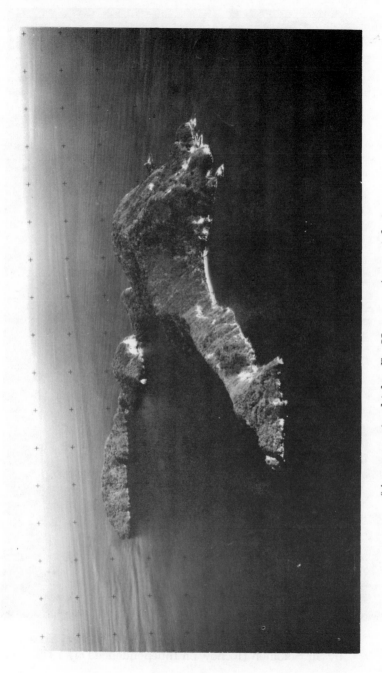

"A penny-sized island" - Huevos.   An aerial view.

Huevos, from the south - mountain, beach and sea.

J.N.Harriman & Co. 61 Marine Square, 1896.

J.N.Harriman & Co. 61 Marine Square, 1922.

Sir Werner & Lady Boos
at a reception for the Prime Minister of the Dutch Antilles.
The menu consisted entirely of local dishes.

Where the fishing is good, and sometimes poor
But a joy not everyone knows.

This heaven on earth with which we are blessed,
Waits patiently each week to greet us.
Where the sea may be calm but sometimes rough -
This little gem is Huevos.

On Carl's sudden death (of haemorrhaging ulcers) in New York in 1931, aged 54, his youngest son Errol Herman Boos (mentioned above) became managing director of Harriman's, at the age of twenty-five, and was ably assisted by his sister Olga. Herman, at the time of his father's death, had been working for nine months with the New Goldfields of Venezuela as a mining engineer, for which profession he had been trained at Lafayette College, U.S.A. With no business training or experience he set about consolidating the business, and with the cocoa trade in an extremely precarious state it was necessary to find other outlets. On the 2nd May, 1932, the firm became a Limited Liability Company, and Herman paid a whirlwind visit to Germany to drum up contacts. He secured the agency for the Horn Line of Steamers and, in 1937, an agreement was made with the firm of Geerz Gebr whereby an exchange of goods was made between the firms on a barter basis. It is interesting to know that it was in their ancestral land that Boos sought to strengthen his commercial contacts; but these were all broken by the start of the Second World War in 1939.

Herman Boos was to manage the firm of Harriman for 44 years and by extremely hard

work, good organisation and reliance on trusted
workers who were to remain with the firm for de-
cades, he more than made up for his lack of business training. When he took over the firm in 1931,
there were less than a score of employees. In 1973,
when the centenary of the firm was celebrated,
Harriman's employed some five hundred people
and had branched out into oilfield equipment, pho-
tographic processing, manufacture of galvanize
and nails, travel agency, insurance and retailing
a great variety of goods from toys to furniture, from
foodstuffs to pharmaceuticals.   There were
branches in Tobago and SanFernando and
Bridgetown, Barbados and a subsidiary in
Kingston, Jamaica. Interestingly enough, in 1951
the firm acquired St Bernard, Lagondoux and La
Cordinière estates, in Mayaro, from the Urich family.

In 1966 the Building Department of the
Firm undertook the complete rebuilding of the old
building. The interior was gutted down to the
sturdy walls, but the old face with its iron gallery,
railings and pillars on the upper floor were retained. The old cocoa house, next door on Chacon
Street, was demolished and replaced by a three-
story building. Also, in 1966 John Harriman Boos,
eldest son of Herman, joined the company and with
his younger brother Robert, who joined the firm
in 1969, represented the fourth generation of the
Boos family to participate in the Company's
growth. Herman Boos died in 1975. He lived to
see his son Robert receive from the Governor-Gen-
eral, in August 1972, the Medal of Merit, Gold, for

Public Service.

The medal was earned as follows. On Wednesday 17th November 1972, a young Trinidadian aged 20, on an Arawak Airlines flight to Tobago, ten minutes before the aircraft was due to land at Crown Point, grabbed the stewardess by the arm, pulled her into the washroom and proceeded to lock it. The passengers glimpsed a knife and a gun. The hijacker then peeped out of the toilet and gave orders to the pilot that he should fly to Cuba, but the Captain replied that he would have to fly to Piarco for refuelling. On landing at the airport, the crew and passengers were allowed to leave, but the hostage, Ms. Gooden, by then in a state of shock, was kept on board the plane. The hijacker was an employee of Harriman's, and hearing of the hijack, Robert Boos soon arrived on the scene. Then, according to the newspapers "a heavy Police party armed with teargas and automatic weapons, nabbed the man as he entered the airport buildings" - escorted by Boos. The Commissioner of Police was a little more discerning than the newsmen, and realised all the credit belonged to Boos, who had first persuaded the hijacker to release the hostage and then brought him in off the plane. He wrote to Robert:

> Your role in effecting her release and the capture of the assailant showed a sense of public duty, courage, resourcefulness, and an understanding of human nature - all attributes which single out a man from a crowd.

The incident also indicated the excellent relations between employer and employee at Harriman's.

The most renowned of Carl Boos' descendants is not however a man, but his daughter Olga. Olga was born at no. 6 Cipriani Boulevard in Newtown, Port of Spain, in 1902, and lived there at the time of her death in 1993, at the age of 91. Olga's early education was received at St. Joseph's Convent Port of Spain. In 1925 she graduated from the College of Mount Saint Vincent, New York, with a Bachelor of Arts degree. After qualifying as a teacher, she returned to Trinidad in 1930, and taught for a short period at Holy Name Convent, in Port of Spain. For twelve years, Olga did voluntary work with the Blind Welfare Association and also helped with the establishment of the School for Blind Children in Santa Cruz, for she was always ready to assist others. During World War II she engaged in serving with the Red Cross Association and the Trinidad and Tobago Tuberculosis Association.

In 1940 Olga joined the family firm of Harriman of which she always remained a shareholder and director, though in 1975 she retired from active association with the firm. In 1948 she was married to A.S.Mavrogordato, a former Commissioner of Police in Trinidad and Tobago, who also joined the firm until his death in 1964. She and her husband were kindred spirits, with a bit of militancy in their character, straight-talking and forthright in what they had to say, though Olga could also be sharp at times. With 'Mavro' as she called him, Olga travelled extensively. She

had a special love for France and the United States
of America but less so for Germany. She was perhaps a little more proud of her French heritage,
through the Rostants, one of Trinidad's foremost
French creole families, than of her German ancestry, though she was equally kind and loving to
all her cousins. Indeed she was very fond of children and a born teacher, and her kindliness made
learning a pleasant experience for them.

With her husband, she translated from the
French the second volume of Pierre Gustave Louis
Borde's, *The History of the Island of Trinidad under the Spanish Government (1498-1797)*. She was
intensely interested in Trinidad's history, began
to collect what eventually became a marvelous collection of books on Trinidad and to do a considerable amount of research on her own.

On her retirement from Harrimans in 1975,
after a great deal of persuasion from her family
and friends, Olga collated the fruit of her quarter
century of research and published in 1977, at her
own expense, *Voices in the Street*, a book on various aspects of Port of Spain's history, (dealing in
a special way with the main buildings of Port of
Spain), that has done more than any other liter-
ary work to stimulate pride in Trinidad's heritage
and to interest Trinidadians of all walks of life in
their past. In the years that followed, she became (in the words of one secondary school student) 'a national resource', and was frequently
called on for help by budding authors. Olga however maintained that students should not be
spoon-fed, should not be carried on the backs of

others, but should learn to do their own work, so that though she gladly helped the industrious, (being a great conversationalist and an excellent teacher), she deftly evicted those who wanted only to exploit her knowledge.

Over these years she also assisted in the production of the following books: *Parish Beat* and *Called to Serve* by Marie Therese Retout O.P.; *Rays of Hope* by Dr. William Dhanessar, cancer specialist; *The U-Boat War in the Caribbean* by Gaylord Kelshall and *From Colonial to Republic - One hundred and fifty years of Business and Banking in Trinidad and Tobago (1837-1987)* and finally the publication she had longed for for many years, that of the two volumes of Borde's History of Trinidad (the first volume translated by James Alva Bain). She was also of invaluable help to a number of historians writing on Trinidad, supplying both research material and also some photographs.

Even though she was well over 85, Olga continued to drive her car and had her time fully occupied, with reading - historical books mainly, - the care of her relatives and particularly the maintenance of her beautiful ancestral home, of which she wrote on the 16th July 1990, the night of the Coup, when fires were raging throughout Port of Spain, and the sound of gunshots was echoing in the streets.

> This house I love is part of me
> For fourscore years has sheltered me
> Where first my eyes beheld the world
> Through spacious rooms and galleries bold
> Where children played so happily

And I myself, my very soul
Became her child for evermore.

Now as we both grow weak for the world
So vastly changed from days long gone
The spirit of this house lives on
Until in time God's will is done.

She would say: "Though I live alone, I am never lonely". But her last years were bedeviled by illnesses of various sorts, necessitating a number of operations. She faced up to all this completely without self-pity, with courage and resilience. She had her own special way of relating to God, and finally when she was 91 decided that her time had come. She died on the 24th April 1993. She was an outstanding example of patriotism and love of country. With her death, it seems unfortunately, that the house she loved, and which is truly a treasure to Trinidad, will have to go.

Olga's uncle, Julius, born just one year after her father, and educated in Germany, worked at first in the family firm of Harriman, in the agricultural sector, but he soon left to run his own cocoa estate at Rio Claro. After sowing his wild oats, he married Audrey Hobson, whose mother was a Rostant and she bore him nine children, which did not particularly please old Karl, as he foresaw financial difficulties. He was even more displeased when Julius on the occasion of the First Holy Communion of one of his sons, decided to become a Catholic. Julius was never a very wealthy man, (although he did manage to send his first son Carl Julius to be educated in the

States, where he remained ever since), so that when he died at the age of forty-eight, his family were left in severe financial straits.

The older boys Oscar and Werner had no chance to further their education but entered immediately into the world of work. Oscar married Gwen Farmer, and worked at Point-a-Pierre. In a bizarre and unfortunate series of incidents at the start of the Second World War, Oscar who was very critical minded, spoke out strongly in public on a number of occasions against the British war effort and was even reputed to have clipped his heels together and given the 'Heil Hitler' salute. In the climate of hysteria then existing, he was reported to the authorities and interned at the St James Barracks, the only one in his family to undergo this ordeal. Of his two sons, Julius was involved in petroleum production, while Hans did magnificent work in building up the Zoological Gardens in Port of Spain.

On his father's death, Werner, who was not yet eighteen and had just finished his Higher School Certificate at St Mary's College, entered the Civil Service. His mother had not even the money to buy him shirts to wear in his new job. He worked in the Colonial Secretary's Office from the age of 17 until he was forty-nine years of age, having then become the Chief Secretary (the equivalent of the old post of Colonial Secretary). In 1956 Eric Williams came to power and for reasons which it is easy to guess, Williams insisted that Werner be removed from office and special arrangements were made for him to retire at that

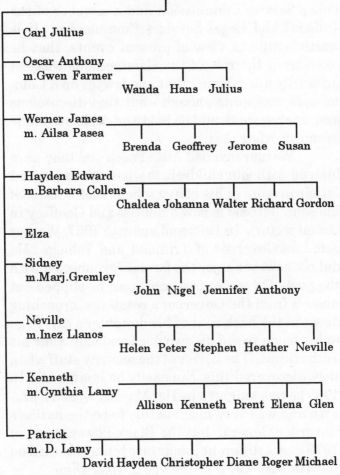

Julius Edward Boos
(1878-1926)
married
Audrey Hobson

Carl Julius

Oscar Anthony
m.Gwen Farmer

   Wanda Hans Julius

Werner James
m. Ailsa Pasea

   Brenda Geoffrey Jerome Susan

Hayden Edward
m.Barbara Collens

   Chaldea Johanna Walter Richard Gordon

Elza

Sidney
m.Marj.Gremley

   John Nigel Jennifer Anthony

Neville
m.Inez Llanos

   Helen Peter Stephen Heather Neville

Kenneth
m.Cynthia Lamy

   Allison Kenneth Brent Elena Glen

Patrick
m. D. Lamy

   David Hayden Christopher Diane Roger Michael

age. By way of compensation, he was made Chairman of the Public Service Commission and of the Police Service Commission and a member of the Judicial and Legal Services Commission. It is worth noting in view of present events, that he considered the role of the Commissions was not primarily a legal one - that one lawyer on a Commission was quite enough - but that discussions and interviews should be held and decisions made promptly after that.

Werner married Ailsa Pasea and they were blessed with four children, to whom he was a good father in spite of his heavy schedule of work. (Of his sons, Jerome is now a dentist and Geoffrey in the oil sector). In 1962 and again in 1967, Werner acted as Governor of Trinidad and Tobago. He did not however enjoy the formality connected with the post. On one or two occasions, he slipped out unseen from the Governor's residence, crouching down in the back seat of his daughter's car, to go to his home to see his two dogs and look after his anthuriums. The horror of the security staff when they discovered this, can easily be imagined! In 1965 he was knighted by Her Majesty Queen Elizabeth and was very much in line to be the nation's Governor General, but the Black Power rising of 1970 cast a different colour on events. He died on the 4th May 1974, at the age of sixty-three.

Werner's brother, Hayden, died young and his wife remarrying - Ronald Greene - the children took their step-father's surname and all live in England. Of his brother Sidney's children (see family tree page 191). John became a missionary-priest in the White Fathers working for very many years in difficult missions in Africa and being at present in a house of Religous formation in the United States; Nigel is a petroleum engineer and Anthony in business. Neville's children are in the business world in Trinidad. Julius' last two sons, Kenneth and Patrick married two sisters, Cynthia and Dolly Lamy and emigrated to Venezuela.

The Boos family were relative latecomers on the Trinidad scene but became Anglicised and Catholicised more rapidly than the other German creole families, undoubtedly because of the continuing breakdown of social and religious barriers in the Trinidad of the early twentieth century, when questions of nationality and religion (and later, race) were becoming subordinate factors to education and wealth.

Chapter 6

Leonard Joseph Graf

*A teacher who can arouse a feeling for one single
good action, for one single good poem, accom-
plishes more than he who fills our memory with
rows and rows of natural objects, classified with
name and form.*

Johann Wolfgang Von Goethe.

Father Leonard Joseph Graf, Holy Ghost
Father of St.Mary's College, Port of Spain, was a
legend in his lifetime, and the length and brilliance
of his priestly career at the school eclipses the
achievements of the many other Germans who
laboured there. So it comes as a surprise to almost everyone, to know that of the fifty priests
who served at St.Mary's College from its foundation in 1863 till its Golden Jubilee in 1913, sixteen (including two Principals) were German, or
to be more precise (most) were Alsatian, that is,
inhabitants of Alsace.

Alsace is a district about twice the size of
Trinidad, consisting of a broad plain bounded on
one side by the river Rhine (which separates it
from modern Germany) and on the other by the
Vosges Mountains. It is one third forested and its
capital and chief city is Strasbourg. The Alsatians
spoke a German dialect, French being found only

in the large towns. Originally part of Gaul, for seven centuries Alsace was under German domination. In 1800 it was French and the very largely Catholic population were strongly Francophile. The Emperor Napoleon said of them: *Let them speak in German, as long as they fight in French.* Alsace was ceded to Germany in 1871, after the Franco-Prussian War but incorporated in France in 1919, after the defeat of Germany in the First World War. In the 1920's when the French Government was very anti-Catholic, there was a movement for independence, but the province remained under France till retaken by Germany in 1939. From 1945 to the present, it has been part of France.

It was in Strasbourg that a Jewish convert to Catholicism, Francis Mary Paul Libermann, was ordained a priest. In 1848 he became the Superior General of the Holy Ghost Fathers, a missionary Order which was partly based in France proper and partly in Alsace, so that when in 1862 the Archbishop of Port of Spain, Ferdinand English, asked the Holy Ghost Fathers to found a secondary school for boys in Trinidad, one of the two priests who opened the College on the 1st August 1863 was an Alsatian, Fr. Albert Sundhauser, and in subsequent years many of his countrymen (and also Germans from further east) were sent out to staff the College in Trinidad.

The names of these German priests, their town of origin, date of birth, and the years that they worked in Trinidad are given below:

Albert Sundhauser, 1837, Ackenheim, Alsace;   1863-1873.
John Muller, 1833, Liebentzwiller, Alsace;   1863-1870.
Francis X. Corbet, 1836, Hochfelden, Alsace;   1867-1874.
Casimir Marcot, 1838, Neuve-Eglise, Alsace;   1869-1876.
Robert Richartz, 1847, Berlin, Prussia;   1874-1878.
Anthony Binder, 1845, Markolsheim, Alsace;   1874-1880.
Joseph Lux, 1854, Wissenbourg, Alsace   1877-1881.
Charles Klein, 1853, Ammerschwir, Alsace;   1880.
John Goettner, 1854, Neuwied, Rhineland;   1880-1885.
John Schmitz, 1853, Aachen, Rhineland.   1881-1890.
Frederick Kurmann, 1854, Munster, Westphalia;
                                          1884-1890.
Emile Allgeyer, 1856, Rixheim, Alsace;   1885-1896.
Hubert Putz, 1858, Burtscheid, Rhineland;   1886-1897.
Charles Wilhelm, 1870, Oderen, Alsace;   1894-1899.
Peter Leimann, 1862, Burtscheid, Rhineland;   1895-1933.
Joseph Spielmann, 1844, Bergheim, Alsace;   1897-1901.
Alphonse Zindt, 1873, Soulzbach, Alsace;   1903-1923.
Leonard Graf, 1883, Aachen, Rhineland;   1905-1970.
Aloyse Haegy, 1878, Ammerschweier, Alsace;   1905-1910.
Joseph Iehl, 1870, Artolsheim, Alsace;   1910-1915.
Charles Meyer, 1881, Wolxheim, Alsace;   1921-1925.

Of the priests listed above, Francis Xavier Corbet and Casimir Marcot, both-French speaking Alsatians, were Principals of St.Mary's College, the first named from 1867-1874, and during this period, the College made the transition from a French school to an English college and became government subsidized; the second being Principal from 1874-1876, and during his administration the school moved across Pembroke street from the old St.George's College buildings, to the present site of St.Mary's College.

John Edward Schmitz was an apprentice carpenter in his father's trade. He entered the

Holy Ghost Fathers' junior seminary at Marienstatt, in 1869. Prince Otto Von Bismarck, the 'Blood and Iron' Chancellor of Prussia (Germany), enforcing an anti-Catholic policy known as the *Kulturkampf,* closed the seminaries in Germany in 1872, and expelled the Holy Ghost priests, who he declared were Jesuits in disguise. The young Schmitz was then sent to Rockwell College, in Tipperary, Ireland to complete his studies. During his years of study, on visits to his homeland he persuaded numerous young men to join the Holy Ghost Congregation, including Peter Leimann, who came to Rockwell in 1874 with half-a-dozen others from the Rhineland. Peter was at the top of his class, excelling especially in the classics but at the same time developing his talents in music and painting. He earned quite a reputation as a rugby player. After ordination to the priesthood he taught at Rockwell for five years and then at his own request was transferred to St Mary's College, Trinidad, where he was joined later by his cousin Leonard Graf, whom he had encouraged to enlist in the Congregation and who followed closely in his footsteps. He died of cancer, in Trinidad in 1933.

The priests listed above, were assigned to St.Mary's College, but a number of them worked also in the parishes. The first parish accepted by the Congregation was that of Diego Martin, in 1870, because the Archbishop was unable to get any diocesan priest to take the parish, since (in the words of Fr. Bouyer) there had been 'sacrilege' (the killing of a priest) in that parish, 'which all

attribute to immorality' (on the part of the priest).
This parish stretched from Diego Martin to
Chacachacare, and the presbytery on this little
island was used as a holiday house by the Holy
Ghost Fathers, who ministered to the 300 people
who were resident there up to around 1900. The
Holy Ghost Fathers also helped with the Calvary
Chapel (seating 100 people) at the foot of
Laventille Hill and just a hundred yards from the
College, and with the St.Joseph parish, in
Trinidad's old capital.

In addition to the German priests, a number of young men, aspirants to the priesthood, were
sent out to 'prefect' at the College from 1865 till
about 1910. They taught there and assisted with
the supervision of the boarders, the discipline and
extra-curricula activities. Unfortunately we do not
have full information on all of them: Muller from
Alsace (1869-72); Schumacher, Holtzeim,
Rhineland (1873-77); Meister (1893-95); Dammers
(1908-1910); Leonard Graf (1905-1910).

Finally, a number of German brothers
played an important role at St Mary's College, in
the building and maintenance of the school and in
technical education. They are listed below:

Theodore Fritsch, 1841, Lampertheim, Alsace; 1863-1897.
Cassien Vincent, 1869, Mulhouse, Alsace;   1889-1890.
Vincent Hodruss, 1887, Zell, Wurttemberg;   1909-1929.
Benno Casper, 1879, Cologne, Westphalia;   1924.
Florian Nieveler, 1879, Duren, Rhineland;   1924.

Brother Theodore gave 34 years of his life
to St.Mary's College, acting as bursar and prefect

at the same time, skilled in calligraphy, music, drawing, painting, plastering, castering and other trades. He was transferred to St.Martial's College, Haiti, in 1897. Brother Vincent was in charge of the infirmary for the boarders and served competently and with painstaking accuracy in administrative duties for close on twenty years. He died from blood poisoning, when the purple ink from a stamp-pad got into a cut on his face. Brother Benno was a construction worker and smith when he entered the Congregation. In 1924, along with Brother Florian, a skilled carpenter, he was sent to Trinidad, to complete the northern wing of the College (bounding the 'Big Yard' on the east).

Leonard Joseph Graf was born in the early hours of Saturday morning, February 10th, 1883, in the town of Aachen in the westernmost part of Germany near the Belgian frontier.

Aachen was an important city from Roman times and was made the northern capital of his empire by the Emperor Charlemagne in the 9th century. Charlemagne tried to make it a worthy capital of his empire and there are still remains of some buildings from his time. The Cathedral in Aachen houses Charlemagne's throne and tomb and was the site of the coronation of many of the Holy Roman Emperors. The town is steeped in history and tradition.

Following the custom of the time, the young Graf, the first-born of his family, was baptised the day after his birth. His family was solidly middle-class and staunchly Catholic. His father was the choirmaster of a choral society in Aachen, and

ensured that all his family - four sons and five
daughters received a good education. From very
early in his life, Leonard felt called to the priesthood; but in the Germany of his time the sense of
freedom and individual independence had been
critically weakened by *Realpolitik* (pure power
politics) and *Interessenpolitik* (politics of material
interest) and the Roman Catholic seminaries had
been closed by the all-powerful Chancellor Otto
Von Bismarck. Over a quarter of the parishes were
without parish priests. In this atmosphere, and
on the advice of his cousin Leimann, the young
Graf at the tender age of ten was sent to the Junior Seminary of Rockwell College, in Tipperary Ireland, to begin his studies for the priesthood with
a view to entering the Holy Ghost Congregation,
which before its expulsion from Germany in 1872
had operated a number of Houses not too far from
Aachen.

Rockwell (situated in the countryside, three
miles from the magnificent ruins of ancient
Cashel), under the guidance of Dr. Crehan, later
Principal of St.Mary's College Trinidad, was one
of the leading schools in Ireland in a very competitive era. The system of studies and honours
and financial remuneration -'payment by results'
- existed in Ireland, and young Graf flourished in
this competitive environment, once he had mastered the English language. Part of the College
(it was a boarding school) was reserved for the junior seminarians, who were under a very prayerful
and strict regime. On the Feast of Corpus Christi,
1894, when he was eleven years of age, Leonard

made his First Holy Communion at Rockwell College, and the following week he was Confirmed by the Bishop of Cashel at the nearby parish church of New Inn. In 1895, the public examination results saw Rockwell with 17 prize winners, only 3 of whom were junior Seminarians, one being young Graf. It soon became obvious to all that the studious German was an exceptionally brilliant student and he ended his secondary studies by winning the first place in the whole of Ireland in the Leaving Certificate Examinations.

Leonard Graf then taught - prefected - at Rockwell College for five years from 1899-1904. He not alone taught classes but was also responsible for discipline among the boys. In addition, during this period he distinguished himself as an *autodidact* (self-taught person) of the first order, by externally taking an Honours Degree in the classics (Greek and Latin) at the Royal University of Ireland (now the National University). He boarded at Blackrock College while sitting the examinations. The degree of Bachelor of Arts was conferred on him on Friday 30th October 1903. During his teaching period at Rockwell, Graf was an active member of the College orchestra and a regular representative player in the scrum of the Rockwell Rugby Team, which competed in the Munster Senior competitions. In these formative years, he had as his fellows Thomas McDonagh, who was to be one of the leaders of the 1916 anti-British rising, and Eamon De Valera future President of Ireland. Not surprisingly, Leonard never acquired, in Ireland, a great love for the English.

In 1905 the Holy Ghost Fathers set up the first novitiate for English speakers, at Prior Park, Bath, England, and Graf went there to do his novitiate or spiritual year. His fellow novices were all Irish and the superior of the House was Dr. John T. Murphy, who had prefected in Trinidad. At the end of the novitiate, Graf took his vows of poverty, chastity and obedience in the Congregation of the Holy Ghost, and was assigned to prefect in Trinidad, partly because of health problems, since it was felt that the tropical climate would assist him towards a speedy recovery.

He arrived in Trinidad on Friday the 27th October 1905, and was conveyed in a horse and buggy to St.Mary's College, just a mile away from the wharf. He was immediately 'thrown to the wolves' - put to supervise the rambunctious boys in the small study, in the period immediately after lunch. Sixty-five years later, one of the mischievous students still remembered Mr Graf:

> On the first day that Mr Graf presided over "Study", rain fell heavily. Here was a new prefect some thought , who did not know the names of his charges, here was Jupiter Pluvius in full force - what better opportunity for some fun and games. So it began with a faint noise which grew in intensity and went on intermittently. Mr Graf must have heard the disturbance but he showed no sign that he had. The following day rains again obliged and the noise continued and again Mr Graf seemed unconcerned. On the third day he broke his silence and said that during the previous days certain boys had been amusing themselves and he wanted them to give him their

names. Some complied readily but others did not. However, when he thought he had collected a sufficient number, he sent them to the Dean and they were severely punished. When I left school Mr Graf was still a prefect but he had already established himself as a successful teacher and strict disciplinarian.

Mr. Graf had a very busy time. Classes (which normally continued till 4 o'clock) were held every day of the week, including Saturdays. The prefects took turns to supervise the boarders' dormitory and the study at night, and woke up the boys before dawn to swim in the plunge pool at the eastern side of the College. Then they had to teach a full day's class and possibly supervise games in the afternoon. The religious were almost never out of their heavy, hot, black soutanes and both priests and prefects alike were called "Fa" (short for Father), and the prefects were expected to be always on call. Along with this demanding schedule, Mr. Graf had to teach himself his studies for the priesthood. But he was a very hardworking and well organised young man, and after two years he had completed his courses in Logic and Philosophy. During the following two years he made great inroads into his theology studies and received tonsure and Minor Orders, on the 24th July 1909.

In 1910 he was sent from Trinidad to Chevilly in France where he attended classes in theology for nearly a year. He was made a subdeacon at Chevilly, on the 2nd October 1910, ordained a deacon a fortnight later, and became a priest forever on the 28th October. He returned to Trinidad on the 26th September 1911, having spent some time at his parents' home at Aachen.

When he began his teaching career at St.Mary's College, Fr. Graf's subject area was the Classics (Latin, Greek and Ancient History). Ray Dieffenthaller wrote concerning him: "I cannot forget my first day at the College. It was in January 1913. My first teacher was Fr. Graf and on that day the subject he taught was Greek. It was not easy, but he was such a lovable gentleman; he was a man of God, a very good teacher, a real scholar". Later on as the need arose, Fr. Graf also taught French; and all these subjects up to the Higher Certificate or Advanced Level and if need be to very large classes, 20 boys and over (even when, in after years, it involved the practical subjects like Botany and Zoology).

Shortly after his arrival, he began work on a fifty years' commemorative magazine for the golden anniversary of St.Mary's College, which was published in 1913. He then became the initiator of the College Annual (Yearbook), which first appeared in 1915, and he continued on as compiler and editor until 1935. This could be a very difficult work, as in the early years the pictures were sent away to Europe to have printing plates of them made. In 1936, he was the editor of the Centenary Record Edition of the Sisters of St Joseph of Cluny, that is, St.Joseph's Convent. Finally, Fr. Graf edited the Centenary Edition of the College Annual, in 1963. There certainly must be few people who can lay claim to editing both a fifty-year edition and a centenary edition of any given

Father Peter Leimann C.S.Sp. 1862 - 1933.

Leonard Graf and his sister at Aachen.

Holy Ghost Community outing to Diego Martin Presbytery (1908)
Back Row: (l.to r.) Fr Leimann, Fr Duggan, Mr J.Leleal,
Fr Brannigan, Br Auguste, Fr J.O'Brien.
Middle: Fr R.Dooley, Fr Neville, Fr O'Donoghue
Front: Mr G.Butler, Br Tobias, Mr L.Graf.

A Family picture at Leonard's ordination to the Priesthood. Leonard is 2nd from left. One of his brothers was also a priest. His father had died a short time before this picture was taken.

publication.

In the early years of the century there was a great need at St.Mary's College for a qualified science teacher. Fr. Graf by dint of persevering and unrelenting study soon qualified himself! He became an extraordinarily skilled teacher in both Botany and Zoology and an acknowledged expert in Trinidad in the taxonomy or recognition and classification of plants in the field. For over fifty years Fr. Graf taught Botany and Zoology to the students of St.Mary's with great success. During this period, for the 42 years that the science scholarship was offered, St.Mary's students won it 31 times. More importantly, both in literature and above all in science, he could impart a love of the subject which has remained with many of his past students. He would wax enthusiastic over the discovery of some tiny plant, or at the sight of some tree-top vine, greeting it like an old friend - "Ah", he would say, *"Doxantha unguis-cati.* Now, now, note the claw-like tendrils - which is why the plant is called 'cat's claw'. Examine the flower. Mmm, well? Is it protogynous or protandrous?"

To teach the botany class about the different types of environment and adaptations of the vegetation, Fr. Graf made regular trips to Mt. Tucuche, the Aripo Savanna, and Monos Island. A student writing in 1936 describes a trip with him to Mount Tucuche:

> Towards the end of the Easter vacation last year, Father Graf according to his usual custom organised an expedition to Mt. Tucuche, the second highest mountain peak in Trinidad.

The party was organised ostensibly to enable the
science students of the Higher Certificate form
to inspect some of the flora that they had been
studying during the previous term but, as usually happens on such occasions, a few unscien-
tific laymen were permitted to accompany us.

We made an early start, not exactly in the cold
grey hours of the morning but early enough to
spoil my beauty sleep. The mode of conveyance
was by bus. The majority of the party amused
themselves on the way by singing and making
loud noises, no doubt evidence of their primitive
ancestry.

On arriving at the foot of the trail we disembarked. Our first halt was a small rest house
just above the valley from which we could just
discern the marvelous view which was to thrill
us so much when we arrived at the top. At about
9.30 a.m. we began the long and difficult ascent.
The guide hewed a way for us through thick tropical undergrowth until we reached the main road
to the peak. We had taken a short cut through
the high woods and so cut six miles off the ascent.

The rest house on the mountain top was not in
very good condition, but we made it do and soon
disposed of the food supply and then drank some
of the ice-cold water found in a barrel at the side
of the rest house. On the way up Fr Graf had
been telling us about the lianes and orchids and
palms and lichens that abound on the mountain-
side, and his short talks afforded great pleasure
to the botanical students who were able to listen
to him. I was (due to exhaustion) in no condition
to do so. After lunch we went further afield and
learned some more about the tropical plants peculiar to mountain-sides like that of El Tucuche.
At 3.30 we started on our downward journey
which was of a much easier and enjoyable na-

ture. Father Graf had his little movie camera with him and interrupted his short talks on the flora in an effort to get snaps of the members of the party sliding down the paths. These snaps provided some comic relief during one of the weekly educational film nights at the College. At about 4.30 we arrived safely at the bottom of the track and then went on to bathe in the river at St Joseph's. At 7 p.m. we were back in Port of Spain after an enjoyable day's outing.

Fr. Graf made eleven trips to the top of Tucuche, the last when he was aged 72. He did, too, all the ordering of scientific equipment for the school, and the laboratories under his care were the best organised in the island. He made his scientific knowledge available also to the Field Naturalist society. The Club had lapsed into a state of dormancy, but upon its revival in 1924, Fr. Graf was among the first to join. The minutes of Friday 3rd October 1924 record that, "On the motion of the Chairman, seconded by Mr Broadway, the Reverend Father Graf was elected a Resident Member". His contribution to the life of the Club took many forms as he organised excursions and was a frequent lecturer, continually exhibiting interesting specimens at meetings. He became a vice president and finally President in 1940, serving in this post until the end of 1945. He was elected an honorary member in 1955, as a mark of appreciation of his services to the club and to scientific education in Trinidad.

From 1920 to 1957, Fr. Graf was dean of Studies for the whole school, having previously for many years been dean of discipline. At one time,

he personally every week reviewed and signed the
judgement book (record of the week's marks) of
each boy, when the roll of St.Mary's was well past
the 800 mark. He also made every effort to check
that teachers assigned and corrected work and
that the boys cooperated fully with the teachers.
Occasionally, he gave a previously unseen passage
to his Higher Certificate Greek class to translate,
or would leave his zoological boys to their dissec-
tions and he would go on his rounds visiting the
classes, chiefly the delinquent ones. As a past student wrote:

> I could see him walking along the galleries at St
> Mary's with measured stride, his keys striking
> up a musical jingle in his pocket. As he entered
> a classroom the boys would immediately rise. He
> would motion them to sit. For a brief moment he
> would survey the class and then turn to the pro-
> fessor and ask, "Well Father, how have these boys
> been doing?" If the report was unfavourable his
> stern countenance would give way to a sardonic
> smile. "So that's it eh. Well I have something in
> my room that will take care of that".

> By now he was speaking in measured tones and
> with greater deliberation than ever, his beetled
> brows riding on the rippling furrows of his fore-
> head. He would turn to the complaining profes-
> sor. Now his black pencil, baton like was beat-
> ing a measured tempo on his left index finger in
> characteristic fashion. "Well Father, if this con-
> tinues give me their names for long penance."
> With this he would leave a chastised classroom
> to visit another that needed to be disciplined, to
> go back to his own classes to be followed by a
> session in his room as dean.

Fr. Graf was a very strict disciplinarian - discipline not for discipline's sake but in order to help the boys. Sometimes reminded by a past student of the not infrequent visits to his room to be disciplined, Fr. Graf had a way of wreathing his face in smiles and throwing back his head, and as he indulged in a quiet laugh, he would say :"At any rate neither of us is the worse for it".

Fr. Graf used corporal punishment when he felt it was necessary, generally on the hand, wielding his cane almost effortlessly and entirely by wrist movement alone and yet hundreds of past students will testify that no Dean had ever wielded a more effective cane, even though he never did so through malice or vindictiveness. In very occasional cases punishment was applied to the seat of the pants. Typically Fr. Graf would tell the erring student: "Touch the chair". The student would place his hands on the top rail of the chair, and Fr Graf would add: "Touch the bottom, not the top", followed by immediate action as the student bent over.

Fr. Graf's moderation is best understood when it is remembered that extremely severe corporal punishment after the English model was still applied in Trinidad. Emilio Borberg, who attended St.Mary's College from 1930 until he was expelled, at age 14, in 1932 (having repeated form 3 - the equivalent of the modern form 1) gives graphic descriptions of his punishments and his contacts with Fr. Graf. On one occasion (of the very many) when he visited the dean, matters went somewhat as follows:

"Give me your billet," (a written description of
the offence committed).
"No, Fah, I don't have no billet. Mr Gaffikin (an
Irish 'Prefect') told me to come up."
"What did Mr Gaffikin send you up for?"
"I bus' Cantaf's mout' for callin' Bitodi a niggah"
The priest closed his eyes, raised his face to the
ceiling ... and seemed to be praying for something.
"You may leave".

But the Principal, Father J.J.English (a
man extremely hard on himself and exceedingly
hard on others) did not deal so kindly with Emilio,
who was incorrigible.

The Father start to flex his arm and the canes.
You hear *swish* - and that is a thin one. Then
you hear *woom*. When you hear *woom*, that is
the Meat Mauler. A thick bamboo rod about four
feet long. Now see if you get the picture. The
pious ---- has you bending over a desk, bare-arse,
blind with fear; then he deals you the first one
with the Mauler. The first is the worst. But I
didn't make a sound, *nada*! In all, you get a dozen
or more welts that seep little drops of blood on
your khaki pants. Man, you can control not making a sound but you can't control the tears and
you can't control your bladder.
And when I got home and my father got home,
and he learned I had been expelled, he gave me a
thrashing with a leather strap on my raw back-
side.

And Borberg tells too, how Fr. Graf (unwit-
tingly) helped to give him some self esteem (which
was badly needed, since even his friends fondly

called him either *Bobes* or *German caca-poule*).

Still later on, he discovered the College library.
Fr Graf was the librarian and also the Dean of
Studies. Behind his thick glasses, this priest was
a laconic mystery to all the boys. Only once, after scores of canings and dozens of transactions
at the library, did he get an inkling of another
facet of Fr Graf's personality. Previously, whenever he had seen Graffie, he was either saying
Mass, caning somebody, or handing out books in
the library.

One day he was crossing the concrete tennis
courts that made up the Big Yard, when the
Priest called him over. He was standing near to
the rope that hung from the belfry; the belfry
was about three stories high, so this was one hell
of a long yellow rope. He was always hoping they
would let him toll the Angelus with that long rope,
but only a few of the Senior boys were allowed to
do it. It had to go stroke-perfect all over the Parish and no junior was capable of that; but he was
damn sure he could do it.

He crossed the courts and when he was near
enough, he said "Yes Fah?"

The Priest was another person altogether. He
was smiling as if he was handing out a
giftwrapped parcel to a deserving boy. He
beamed. "Would you like to act in the play this
year?"

The boys knew that every year it was a different
Shakespeare play, and there would be parts like
Cassius or Romeo or Mark Anthony and even the
black fella Othello. Man, black is white, he would
take any of those parts; Boy! He would get up on
that stage...

"Sssure, Fah", whichever you pick for me..."

"You may have noticed in the other plays, that

there are usually two or three maidens standing
around..."
"What!?"
"As I was saying, these maidens have very little
to say..."
"Wait a minute, Fah..."
"We use these maidens to balance the stage col-
orfully..."
"Not with me, Fah, sorry".
"What do you mean not me, not you? Haven't
you seen the other boys doing it every year?
"Yes Fah, I've seen those fellas." His throat hurt
with the disappointment and he hung his head
for a moment. "You mean to put on a dress and
lipstick and rouge, and try to look like a girl..."
"The other boys do it!"
"Not this boy, Fah."
"Well, if that's the case, I'm very sorry". Not
smiling any more, he took back his present and
walked away.
The boy was anxious and grateful, so he called
out to the departing Priest, "Thank you Fah,
thanks a lot!" And he muttered to himself, "May
God bless you Father". Because this priest, dear
to many generations, had shown him how to lift
his sights, even if it was only for a fleeting disap-
pointing moment.

Gradually, more and more of the St.Mary's
College students were day boys, and Fr. Graf,
recognising that corporal punishment could now
become a last resort, cut down on it and introduced
a system of Long Penance (detention) sessions for
delinquents, conducted in the Big Study from 4
p.m. to 5 p.m. on some afternoons. His unique
way of conducting the sessions, however, was not
by sitting at a rostrum above the students, but by

walking up and down amongst them for the entire length of the Big Study praying the Divine Office, moving with a slightly swaying gait, blackbound breviary in hand, saying the Latin words with sibilant aspirations. But let no one think he could take advantage of such a situation. Lynx-eyed and as though by some inner sense, he could detect the time wasters, even while at prayer. He would interrupt his prayers, standing over the culprit, and tell him to let him see what he had under the desk. Many a novel and comic book that had no place in detention was detected thus and put away. This long penance became so well known that one carnival the following calypso was sung in the streets of Port of Spain:

> Fr. Graf jovial man
> Give long penance
> whenever he can.
> What yuh did?
> Late to school.
> Long penance.
> What yuh did?
> Las in de class.
> Long penance.
> etc.

The students considered Fr. Graf to be very fair and just, with no favourites, although one student still complains, fifty years after he has left school, that when he was a boarder he smuggled in some mangoes from outside, was caught with them in the dormitory and punished for stealing mangoes from the julie mango trees in the College, while Fr. Graf as a botanist should have been

able to distinguish the college mangoes from those
outside.   Another was punished for stealing
pommecytheres from the tree in the College and
maintained that he got extra punishment because
Fr. Graf dearly loved pommecytheres, giving as
proof the fact that after he left school he sent a
bag of pommecytheres to Fr. Graf and received
special thanks for his gift!

Fr. Graf was a man of very equable tem-
perament, with a quiet sense of humour. On one
occasion a fellow priest remarked to him that "Father B... has certainly a marvelous memory". "Yes"
agreed Fr. Graf, "But he never remembers how
many times he has told the same story".   In his
later days, he could silence erring boys who invented excuses, with: "Now, now, son, your grandfather gave me that excuse. Please try a new one."
Partly because of this sense of humour, he seldom
got annoyed. For instance one day (on the eve of
the football intercol) when he entered the zoology
classroom and saw that the skeleton in the glass-
case was dressed in a St.Mary's College football
jersey, he said simply in his deep voice, "well, well";
on the other hand he was understandably furious
when he found a glass case shattered and the ex-
planation given that a science student had gone
berserk because he had been force-fed a piece of
dog-fish preserved in formaldehyde!

As dean, the boys considered him to be
omnipresent. The sound of his jingling keys coming down the corridor gave them timely warning
and saved him a great deal of trouble - as one past
student expressed it: 'The Graf of the jingling keys

who could silence a misbehaving class from fifty feet'. But though in his early days he seemed also to be all-seeing, he later learned to sometimes look the other way. For example, he never happened to be around the morning the boys brought in the frogs for dissection, and before their chloroformed demise, gave them the opportunity to take part in the great annual frog race down the gallery to the west of the zoology laboratory, to the eager urging of the boys. Because an occasional frog, excessively 'ridden' by its owner, might jump over the bannister to meet an explosive and untimely death on the concrete of the Big Yard far below, it may be supposed that Fr. Graf would be labelled by some tender-hearted moderns as tolerating cruelty to animals; and similarly his corporal punishment of delinquent students would be viewed as 'child abuse' and his long penance as 'a violation of human rights', but one wonders if (as he said) the students of the College were any the worse for it!

From 1912 to 1924, Fr. Graf was in charge of the College choir, which used to prepare suitable pieces for prizegiving and other functions and also assured that the numerous Latin hymns and responsories in the liturgy were presented with due solemnity. He was moreover, a regular member of the College orchestra, being proficient on the cello.

His connection with the Dramatic Club began in 1930, and he produced a play every year for the next 30 years. Generally it was one of Shakespeare's plays, for which the good priest looked after both the production, ordering of the costumes and arrangement of the scenery, and the direction, coaching the actors and even serving as prompter. To his logical German mind, Othello had necessarily to be a black person and the other characters white, so that as a result, generally only white or slightly coloured boys acted in the St.Mary's plays - a procedure which in later, more enlightened times, was held against him.

Fr. Graf was in charge of the boys' Library. He organised the Higher Certificate boys as Library assistants, presided over the loan of books every Friday afternoon, and looked after the ordering of new books and magazines. He was a keen amateur photographer and used to take movies on his botanical excursions and at the College sports. These he would show to the boys on a Friday evening in the College's Big Study (now the Centenary Hall) along with other films designed to educate and amuse - films like Laurel and Hardy, Charlie Chaplin and Popeye shorts.

Fr. Graf's day began at 4.40 a.m. as he rose for Community prayer with the other priests, followed by private prayer till five minutes to six. For very many years he celebrated the public Mass in the College Chapel at 6 o'clock. This, he said, was what he valued most in his life. When it was his turn to say the boys' Mass and to preach on Sundays, his sermons were never long nor eloquent. They were rather simple, direct, down to earth and thought-provoking. After he had a minor stroke, about the age of 75 he no longer said the public Mass on Sundays. After breakfast, Fr. Graf began his full day's work of seven Higher

A Community outing to Maracas Bay. (1920) A rest at the crest.

"As You Like It". Fr.Graf's first play. (1932)

The Cast of "The Rivals", (1961), on an outing to Bellevue.
Top: Fun for all.
Bottom: Fr.Graf and Adrian Camps-Campins.

"The Lion" in his later days.

Certificate classes - Latin, Greek, French, Botany and Zoology - and dean of studies. Then he might have to take Long Penance or Library, followed by practice for the Shakespeare play. However, when at all possible (which was often only on a Sunday) he went for a walk round or through the Queen's Park Savannah, with his white cork hat on his head, in white soutane with swinging black cincture, stopping occasionally to examine some interesting botanical specimen, or quietly saying his rosary, or stopping for a few moments to look at a cricket or football match. If he met any of his students at play, he always greeted them and never discouraged those who chose to walk some of the way with him - though in his younger days he walked too fast for most. Sometimes, his work of correcting exercises or school administration kept him going late into the night but as he grew older, his regularity in everything was remarkable - one could set a clock by his movements and he always retired at 9 o'clock.

When he was 74, Fr. Graf gave up his deanship and took a normal class load of seven subjects a day. When he was 80, this was reduced to 2 periods of Greek a day, to the Higher Certificate class. He taught his last day's class on Thursday 30th June 1966, after which he officially retired from teaching at the age of 83 years, having given 60 years of his life to teaching at St.Mary's College. During these sixty years of teaching, the fact that he missed only two days of class is a testimony not only to his good health but also to his indomitable will. When he suffered so badly from a most painful attack of shingles that sleep was impossible, he spent half the night pacing up and down the Big Yard, and then took his classes as usual the next morning.

He went home to Germany on holiday in 1922, 1934 and 1956, visiting his family and also spending some weeks at Rockwell College, Tipperary, to renew old memories of his boyhood. In 1961, he flew to the States for a prostate operation. But it was the strong bonds of Community life which kept Fr. Graf going. Community outings or occasional excursions were a welcome break. In the long "summer" holiday, Fr. Graf would spend a few days "down the islands" (at Gasparee or Monos) with the community of the Holy Ghost Fathers. He enjoyed his swimming, bridge in the afternoon and a little reading.

Fr. Graf was of middle height. His piercing blue-grey eyes, till they softened with age, seemed to search into one's very soul. His heavy eyebrows and deep purposeful voice and reputation as a disciplinarian were enough to scare any young boy on the first encounter. Yet as time passed one realised that beneath his stern exterior lay a warm, gentle and understanding heart. Over the years the boys called him either 'Graffie' or 'the Lion', a nickname that at once explained his at times leonine appearance (light-haired and ferocious looking) as well as his first name, which was Leonard.

Fr. Graf, during his lifetime and after his death, was described by such titles as 'A Masepesian Rock of Principle, a storehouse of humility, an epitome of justice, an inimitable *fac totum*, a mind of inestimable magnitude, a paragon of learning'. One may ask how did he find time and energy and inspiration to do it all? A modern psychologist might say he was a workaholic with a compulsion to labour but perhaps the reality was different. His unspoken motto was 'service' and his driving force was charity. He never deliberately wasted one minute of his working life, and his work was his enjoyment. He was always devoted to the Sacred Heart of Jesus and promoted the society of that name among the Senior boys. In recognition of this, on the Golden Jubilee of his Ordination to the priesthood, the Past Students' Union erected a stained-glass window to the Sacred Heart in the College Chapel. He had a great confidence in Our Lady, and after the audience had departed from seeing the plays in the College hall, at that late and silent hour of the night he could be seen walking up and down saying his rosary. Yet he never used his position as a teacher to teach religion in class or to make any but the most passing references to religious matters when they arose in the context of what was being studied.

Because he was a German, he was never made Principal of the College. Nevertheless, he was 'the man behind the scenes' in all dealings with the Government with regard to education and in relations with the Superior General of the Holy Ghost Fathers in Paris, with regard to allocation of personnel and particularly in 1931, when the question arose of the closure of St.Mary's College, in order to send more missionaries to Africa. During the first world war, Fr. Graf had to report each day to the authorities, and also for some time at the start of the second. He loved Trinidad and devoted his life to its people but he loved his native land too. Over his long years in Trinidad he kept in touch with his family in Germany. He was desolate when in the second world war, his home town of Aachen was almost bombed out of existence. Though he abhorred the Hitlerian regime, the unconditional surrender of Germany to the Allies in 1945 affected him deeply. But he never told his sorrow to anyone.

It is sometimes said, with regret, that Fr. Graf never left anything in writing, (apart from a couple of articles in the Field Naturalists' magazine), but indeed he did. All the unsigned editorials in the College Annuals up to 1935, were the products of his pen, little jewels of wisdom which are still applicable today:

> We should become alarmed at the shallowness of the young students turned out by schools and colleges where science and mathematical teaching predominates and where the classics are tabooed; no educated citizen can afford to ignore the example of the Romans in uniting, in a contented and prosperous Commonwealth, nations widely differing in race, colour, language and culture... or that of the Greeks with whom originated our conception of political freedom.

> What is demanded in commercial and industrial life is character, breadth of view, judgement, grasp of principle , and the power of clear think-

ing and clear expression. Modern business is a matter of immense complexity, and success in it depends largely on a man's power of dealing with his fellow-men, whether as colleagues, competitors or employees.

The tendency to abandon agricultural pursuits and to allow the land to pass into the possession of outsiders is a deplorable one both for the community and for the individual. This is true for any country, but particularly so for Trinidad.

After his retirement, Fr. Graf spent a great part of his day in deep meditation and prayer. On evenings he could be found in the Oratory saying his Rosary. He received many visits from past students many of whom came to his room for counsel or advice; and it is now known that he had very secretly obtained and given financial assistance to many promising young students whose fathers had died or families had been unable to support their College education. On Sunday 31st August 1969, he was awarded the Chaconia Medal (Gold) in the country's first ever National Awards Presentation for 'Long and meritorious service to Trinidad and Tobago in the sphere of Education'. This presentation was made to him by Dr Eric Williams, the then Prime Minister and was witnessed by Sir Solomon Hochoy, the Governor General and one of the many eminent past students of Fr. Graf.

Fr. Graf's health began to decline to the point where he had to confine himself to the seclusion of his room. On Thursday 15th January 1970, barely able to walk, he was reluctantly removed

from his room to the infirmary on the eastern side
of the College and put under the care of a nurse
who constantly kept watch. At ten minutes to
seven that evening, he died, his left hand clutch-
ing a rosary which he wore around his neck, a gift
from his sister Christine. He was 87 years old.
What Count Finbar Ryan, the Archbishop of Port
of Spain, wrote from Cork, Ireland, on receiving
news of Father Graf's death, is perhaps the best
summation of the priest's long life:

> It is natural that men of the world should stress
> Father Graf's distinction as a man of encyclope-
> dic knowledge, and prince of teachers, an exact-
> ing but just disciplinarian. But for me he was
> first and last, a priest: more perhaps to me than
> even to the members of his Community was his
> growing sanctity evident - his spiritual self
> seemed translucent in his frail body. He was the
> last person I visited on the day of my departure
> from Trinidad.

NOTES AND REFERENCES

The German background was obtained chiefy from: *German Cultural History from 1860 to the present day*, by Nyphenburger Verlagshandlung, and *A History of Germany, 1815-1945*, by William Carr, as well as from a number of articles on specific subjects. No bibliography is given as extensive reading done for the preparation of other books on Trinidad was made use of. References are given for individual chapters.

Chapter 1
The German Community.

Page.

1. Brandenberg & Trinidad - The Europeans in the West Indies, 1493-1688. A.P. Newton.
2. 1797 & German Regiments - History of Trinidad and Tobago., G.Carmichael. pages 44,63, 371-2.
4. "Slow Fevers" - Trinidad Historical Society Documents 11-11-1797.
4. Project to settle Germans - C.Goodridge, Land, labour and immigration into Trinidad 1783-1833. Unpublished Thesis Univ. of Liverpool, 1976.
5. de Boehmler - Family Papers. Urich Diary.
5. Dr.Schaw - G.Carmichael (above) p. 94.
6. Population Census - Trinidad by Daniel Hart.
6. Catholic marriages - R.C.Cathedral Registers.
6. Beat wives - Urich Diary.
6. Leveingstein - No.5 Sept.1989 News Letter from the District Grand Lodge of Trinidad.
7. List of Germans - Urich Diary.
7. Germans in Tdad.1830 - Urich Diary.
8. No 'Crepe' - Wuppermann diary.
9. Letter from liberal - Schoener family.
9. Letter from Seheult - Wuppermann papers.
10. Petition to King - CO 295/96.
11. List of Assessors - Royal Gazette 1838.
11. Gerolds - Olga Mavrogordato.

13. Wuppermann - Wuppermann diary & family papers
15. Feez - Ian Jardine. Père Massé Diary.
16. Prahl - Wuppermann Diary.
16. Zurcher - Ian Jardine for information and quote from newspaper.
17. Von Weiler - Mrs McCarthy.
18. Wehekinds - E.Agostini & Urich Diary.
19. Fanovich - Trinidadiana, Bodu - for Railway accident.
20. Clergymen C.M.S. - G.Carmichael (above) page 227, and archives of Anglican Church.
21. Mass German immigration - G.Carmichael (above) page 416 and T.&.T. Historical Society publication No.1047, June 1967, Migration into Trinidad in the 1840's by C.R.Ottley.
25. Ston Family - East & West Indians Rescue Trinidad, C.R.Ottley pages 27-32.
26. Borberg - Michael Llanos & Borberg Family papers.
27. Roman Catholic Clergy - Archives Archbishop's House.
27. Muller - Massé Diary.
30. Benedictines - Fr. John Pereira O.S.B.
32. German Creole Religious - St.Joseph of Cluny Centenary Record etc.
32. Franciscan Sisters - Archives Archbishop's House.
33. Schoener - Schoener family; Trinidad, Who, Why, What, 1950. Ian Jardine. For Murder - Bodu.
34. Hotel de France - Abbé Massé diaries.
36. French Verse - E.Agostini.
36. Germania Club house - Ian Jardine & Guide to Trinidad, Collens page 69.
37. Vineta - Year Book.
38. Goellnicht - Goellnicht family.
39. Wippenbeck - C.de Freitas.
40. List of technicians etc - Newspaper, Year Books.
41. Hahn - Hahn family; P.O.S.G. 4-4-1906.
44. Nothnagel - Nothnagel family.
48. Gocking - Gocking family.
49. Dieffenthaller - The Life and Times of Ray Dieffenthaller, Selwyn Ryan.
51. Brumer - Lenagan memoirs.

52. El Callao - A Naturalist in the Guyanas, Eugene André. Ch. 3.
53. Meyer - Lady Reece and E.Reichmann.
56. 1st World War internment - Nothnagel papers.
57. Warzes   - Charles Wears.
59. 2nd World War internment - Hans Stetcher Paper in Caribbean Studies by Dona Farah. Tattoos - Fr.A.Dick.
62. Impact of Germans - the author's conclusions.

Chapter 2
The Urich Family

65. Urichs in Germany - Thorisman Wolf.
67. Friedrich in Trinidad - Urich Diary.
69. Marriage Proposal - Urich Diary.
69. Business & Marriages - Urich family and Trinity Cathedral Baptismal Register.
71. Whaling: Request to City Council - City Council Records 1827.
Request to Governor - Trinidad Duplicate Despatches 1834.
Jenny Point - Chaguaramus Assessment Roll 1884.
Description of whaling - Trinidad, L.A.A. de Verteuil.
Song of the Whalers - Trinidad's French Verse, A.deVerteuil.
77. John Urich - Urich family.
78. Paul & Marousha - Urich family.
78. Otto Gottfried - Urich family.
79. Friedrich & Sons - Urich family.
79. Scientific Association - Year Books.
79. Irene & Wilfred - Mrs Wendy Bourne.
80. Otto at school - Gawthorne memoirs - Archbishop's archives.
82. Jangoons - Family tradition.
85. Field Naturalist Society - Field Naturalist Society publications.
88. New species discovered* - Victor Quesnel.

88. Search for Guacharo birds - Memoirs of J.D.Lenagan.
90- Rest of the family - Family tradition.

* The following is a complete list of the all the species discovered by Urich and to which his name was consequently given.

1. Akodon urichi - a mouse
2. Eleutherodactylus urichi - frog
3. Symmachia u. - butterfly
4. Anastrepha u. - a fly.
5. Lygistorrhima u. - a fly
6. Embia u. - a strange little insect that spins webs with silk from glands in the front legs.
7. Natada u. - a moth
8. Waldheimia u. - hymenopteran insect.
9. Xenomymar u. - hymenopteran insect
10. Trissolcus u. - hym. insect
11. Spelaeomyrmex u. - ant
12. Sericomyrmex u. - an ant
13. Apterostigma u. - ant
14. Trachymyrmex u. - an ant
15. Camponotus u. - an ant
16. Paraleyrodes u. - a bug
17. Liothrips u. - a thrips
18. Xyleborus u. - a beetle
19. Psammisia urichiana - a vine of the family Vacciniaceae.

He was originally credited with the discovery of a blind cave-dwelling cat fish (Caecorhamdia urichi) but this name is now invalid since it is now known to be indentical to Ramdia quellen.

Chapter 3
The Stollmeyer Family.

Unless otherwise indicated all material in this chapter comes from the Stollmeyer family papers.

93. Escape from conscription - newspaper report of his death.
95. Scheme with Etzler - Trinidad in Transition, Donald Wood, pages 85-89.

109. Good Templars - Trinidadiana, Bodu, page 32.
111. Peace Union - Trinidadiana, Bodu, page 104.
112. Legislative Council - Legislative Council Papers, Red House Library.
123. Magnificent Seven - Humming Bird 14-9-1904; Mirror, September 1904.
125. Killarney - Voices in th Street, Olga Mavrogordato.
130. Oil disaster - Oil Pioneer, A.Beeby-Thompson, page 127.

Chapter 4
The House of Siegert

Unless otherwise stated material on the Siegert Family comes from Angostura Ltd. Small bits of information have also been obtained from Obituary accounts: Mirror & Port of Spain Gazette October 1903; Humming Bird, 10th June 1905; Trinidad Guardian 24th March 1919; and also from Trinidad Then & Now, J.N.Brierly page 266-9.

138. Angostura - A Naturalist in the Guyanas, Eugène André Ch. 4.
139. Siegert Family - Gordon Siegert.
140. 20 dozen cases - Eversley, Trinidad Reviewer.
142. Charles W.Warner - P.O.S.G. 17-10-1903.
142. El Callao - André (above) page 52.
146. Family marriages - Gordon Siegert.
146. Export Figures - Collens, Guide to Trinidad.
148. Loss of ship "Dr. Siegert" - Auf Weiterfart by Friedrich Spengemann. (See translation opposite picture).
148. Charity to poor - Newspapers as above.
150. The Hall - Voices in the Street, Mavrogordato.
151. Anecdotes about Carlos - Gordon Siegert.
151. Ruthless Businessman - Boos family papers.
153. Anecdotes about Luis - Gordon Siegert.
156. Woodbrook Estate - Voices in the Street, Mavrogordato; The Making of Port of Spain, Michael Anthony Ch.16.

157. "Allies Bay" - Fr. M. O'Dwyer.
160. Inventory - Gordon Siegert.

Chapter 5
The Boos Family.

Unless otherwise indicated all information in this chapter
is from the Boos family papers. Some of that about Olga
Mavrogordato is from Sr. Marie Thérèse Retout O.P.

165. A clerk in those days - Collens, Guide to Trinidad,
     page 31.
166. The Hancox ships - A Naturalist in the Guyanas,
     Eugène André, page 34.
168. Deed of 6th June 1887 - Wuppermann papers.
169. 'Firm was at sea level' - Lenagan memoirs about
     Archer Company.
170. Family home - Architectural details from Adrian
     Camps-Campins.
171. Quote from Mirror - Mirror 4-4-1903.
172. Telephone Co. - Trinidad Reviewer, T.Fitz-Evan
     Eversley.
180. Easter-weekend outing - 18-4-1906 Port of Spain
     Gazette.
180. Occupations at islands - 18-4-1906 Port of Spain
     Gazette.
181. Spanish Galleon - T. & T. Historical Society publica-
     tion no.1046, 21-11-1967, "The Spanish Galleon" by
     R.D.Archibald.
185. Hijack - Newspapers of November 1972.
192. Family Information - Lady Boos.

Chapter 6
Leonard Joseph Graf.

Unless otherwise indicated all material for this chapter was
obtained from the following sources: Oral information from
the Holy Ghost Fathers, Holy Ghost Fathers' archives, St
Mary's College Annuals, article on Fr Graf by Everard Byer.

196. List of priests & brothers - A Spiritan Who was Who, in North America and Trinidad, 1732-1981, Henry J. Koren C.S.Sp.
203. Ordination dates - Archbishop's Archives.
210. Borberg's reminiscences - A copy in the possession of Michael Llanos.

INDEX OF SPANISH PROTOCOLS
1787-1813

The only references in this index (which registers all official business dealings during this period) to persons with German names are as follows:

DIEFFENTHALLER: Joseph: 1798 sale of 2 slaves; 1799 sale of a schooner; 1801 stood security; 1806 sale of 3 slaves; 1809 sale of several slaves; sale of a schooner; sale of a shop or magazine to the Gentlemen Peschier; Joseph D. and Sablich give power of attorney.

Rose D. house sold to 1806; Madame D. and Louisa and Josephina D. sold individual slaves in 1810, 1811 and 1813 and a dower was given to Josephina in 1813.

SABLICH: Anthony: a number of business references from 1803 onwards.

FANOVICH: John: 1808 sale of a lot to John F. and Anthony Navacoviche; sale of a slave to John Fanovich.

SHOULLER (probably Schuler) Francis: 1805 Francis and his wife sold certain slaves; 1810 sale of an estate.

INDEX OF GERMAN NAMES
connected with Trinidad.

ILLUSTRATIONS

Chapter 1:
All pictures are from the families concerned except:
Mrs Mahon: Wuppermann house; Rudy at University.
Miss Elise Agostini: Sampadrura Estate; Easter Card.
Mr Ian Jardine: Blarney, Messrs.A. & L. Schoener.
Mr Adrian Camps Campins: Borberg, Railway Accident,
Trinidad Fencing Club, residence of August Holler.
Wharf at Ciudad Bolivar: Eugène André, a Naturalist in
the Guyanas.

Chapter 2:
All pictures are from the Urich family except:
Aquarella Galleries: Whaling by Cazabon.
Holy Ghost Fathers: South Quay by Cazabon.

Chapter3:
All pictures are from the Stollmeyers except:
Aquarella Galleries: Conrad F. Stollmeyer and Anna
Stollmeyer by Cazabon.
Sketches - three Stollmeyer Residences Gerald C.Watterson.

Chapter 4:
All pictures are from Mr Rene Bermudez, except:
Sketch of Geo. Brown House - Gerald Watterson. Alfred Galo
and dog and caricature of Alfredo C. Siegert - Mr G. Siegert.
Outing at Copperhole - Mr Adrian Camps Campins.
George Street Factory, Exhibition, Ship 'Dr Siegert', Messrs.
Luis B. & Alfred C. Siegert - Angostura Ltd.
Mrs Prinz - Ms E. Agostini.

Chapter 5:
All pictures are from the Boos family.

Chapter 6:
All pictures are from the Holy Ghost Fathers except:
Play outing at Bellevue - Mr Adrian Camps Campins.